Endorsements

"The English verb *to lead* comes from the Indo-European root *leith*, which simply means to step across a threshold. This simple image captures the essence of the everyday acts of heart and courage that Deborah Reidy recounts in her stirring book about what people can and are doing to benefit people with disabilities, including the 'disabled' themselves."

>—Peter Senge, founding chairperson of the Society for Organizational Learning, author of *The Fifth Discipline: the Art and Practice of the Learning Organization*, and coauthor of several other books

"Wonderful, heartful, useful ... Reidy's insights and stories illuminate the meaning of life and the practices of leadership that will improve the quality of life for others."

>—Ron Heifetz, founder of the Center for Public Leadership at Harvard University and author or coauthor of several seminal books on leadership, most recently *The Practice of Adaptive Leadership* with coauthors Alexander Grashow and Marty Linsky

"Deborah Reidy draws upon years of experience in the field to provide readers with an easy-to-read framework of leadership development loaded with practical tips on every page, providing many inspirational stories of citizen leaders and offering readers suggestions on how to get started on the path to personal development."

>—Colleen Wieck, executive director of the Minnesota Governor's Council on Developmental Disabilities of the Department of Administration and the primary creator of Partners in Policymaking, a leadership training program for adults with disabilities and parents of young children with developmental disabilities

"Deborah Reidy offers a reliable guide to strengthening the motivation, understanding, voice, and practices necessary to effective action that serves people's higher purposes. She skillfully brings her readers into the powerful conversations about leadership that currently engage growing numbers of thinkers concerned with a just and sustainable future, clearly describes their practical implications, and provides a series of well-designed exercises that encourage exploration and application."

—John O'Brien, advisor on developmental disability issues in the forefront of innovations in the disability field for many years and the author of numerous books and articles

"Deborah Reidy has written a short and readable book on a question that countless people will ask themselves many times: "Should or could I lead?" Deborah has taken this broad question of leadership and broken it into its various ingredients, providing in each instance a chapter in the book that provides a chance for the reader to read and reflect. She has drawn on her own experiences and that of many others who are involved with issues in the lives of persons with disabilities and the questions of leadership that can arise at any point. It is this attempt to ground leadership in the practical daily life of everyday people that may surprise many, since leadership is often thought of as being far removed from the ordinary challenges of life."

—Michael Kendrick, leadership consultant extensively involved in leadership and change projects in the United States, Canada, Australia, New Zealand, and other countries and the author of numerous articles

Why Not Lead?

A Primer for Families of People with Disabilities and Their Allies

DEBORAH E. REIDY

iUniverse, Inc.
Bloomington

Why Not Lead?
A Primer for Families of People with Disabilities and Their Allies

iUniverse books may be ordered through booksellers or by contacting:

iUniverse
1663 Liberty Drive
Bloomington, IN 47403
www.iuniverse.com
1-800-Authors (1-800-288-4677)

Cover image©Katharine Marshall

ISBN: 978-1-4620-4762-8 (sc)
ISBN: 978-1-4620-4763-5 (e)

Library of Congress Control Number: 2011915503

Printed in the United States of America

iUniverse rev. date: 2/22/2012

In memory of my mother,
whose quiet leadership made such a difference

CONTENTS

ACKNOWLEDGMENTS

Special thanks to the many people with disabilities, their families, advocates, and human service workers who have taught me so much and inspired me over the past three decades. This book truly could not have been written without you.

Thanks also to the people who have regularly asked about my writing and expressed interest in holding a copy of the published book in their hands. This has kept me going even when my enthusiasm waned.

I've been deeply influenced by the work of numerous people in the disability field and beyond. In particular, Wolf Wolfensberger's work profoundly shaped my thinking and actions over the course of my career and set my life on a path that introduced me to many other remarkable leaders. His exacting standards instilled a rigor that I draw upon to this day.

The work of Ron Heifetz offered a conceptual foundation for my earliest thinking about leadership in the public sector and continues to influence my thinking today. I've also been deeply influenced by the work of Peter Senge and other colleagues in the Society for Organizational Learning, who have freely shared what they know about systems thinking, coaching, and how to be a skillful human being in the world.

Several people read chapters and offered comments, but I'd like to thank Matt Rigney in particular. Matt read the entire manuscript and offered detailed comments, suggestions, and encouragement. Rick Karash and Gwen Gosselin each read chapters and offered useful ideas for improvement. John O'Brien offered support and encouragement from the inception of this book. Thanks also to coach Cameron Powell who, at a crucial time, helped to guide me out of the harbor.

As always, I am grateful to my husband, Jim, for seeing capacities in me that I'm only just growing into.

Introduction

Leadership can be exercised by anyone who cares enough. This truth will not be found in most of the popular literature on the topic, because prevailing concepts of leadership favor the talented, the charismatic, the heroic, the people with the title. In fact, leadership is often exercised by ordinary people doing what they care about, but it frequently is unrecognized as leadership. That leaves ordinary people who want to exercise leadership with few relevant examples.

In fact, the human service field is rich with such examples. Sandy, who works tirelessly to design adaptive equipment for people with severe disabilities, wants to broaden her influence on the social environments in which her clients must navigate. She has developed a training event on social integration that she hopes will communicate her ideals, even though she has never considered herself a public speaker. Michael, who believes people with disabilities ought to be able to choose what they eat for dinner, has challenged the policy of the group home where he works, which prescribes standard weekly menus for the residents. Jo, concerned about the safety of vulnerable people in hospital settings, not only advocates for specific individuals, but also works with hospital nurses to help them be better protectors of their patients. Each of these small acts has made a difference in the lives of the people directly affected, has worked toward a vision important to the actors, and yet will rarely be recognized as leadership. In fact, the actors themselves may not recognize their actions as leadership. As a result, these actions may stay in the realm of "random acts of kindness" rather than the beginning of an intentional leadership career.

The aim of this book is to serve as a guide and a resource for caring people as they undertake an intentional path of leadership. Its primary audience is families of people with disabilities and their allies, including people with disabilities themselves, advocates, staff, board members, and others who care deeply about the lives of human service clients. It is informed by the experiences of ordinary people who assumed leadership roles because they cared about a person or a cause and decided to try to make a positive difference.

Through a combination of case studies, short narratives, and personal exercises, I will personally guide you into an enhanced understanding of what leadership is, assist you to strengthen your motivation, and deepen your understanding and application of core leadership attributes and practices.

The content of this book reflects my decades of experience as a leader, as well as being a student and teacher of leaders. I've worked in the human service field since 1976, with the majority of my work aimed at creating conditions where people with disabilities are valued, contributing members of their communities. At the age of twenty-four, I founded a residential agency serving some of the most severely disabled people to live outside institutions at the time. I then founded an innovative program, Education for Community Initiatives (ECI), which offered education and consultation to community members and staff of human service agencies in their efforts to include people with disabilities in all aspects of community life. During the 1980s and early 1990s, ECI's work was very much in the vanguard of the field. There were regular opportunities to bring together leaders from the fields of disability, social justice, education, and other areas for conferences, seminars, and "think tanks."

Upon leaving ECI in 1993, I joined the Massachusetts Department of Mental Retardation (now Department of Developmental Services, DDS) as Director of Training and Development. In this role, I was responsible for organizing a system of training for many thousands of service workers, families, board members, and others. One of the biggest needs was a coordinated strategy to support the leadership development of the staff, families, and service recipients affiliated with the agency. I played a key role in designing and delivering leadership-development programs in Massachusetts and have continued to do so since the mid-90s. This intensive exposure has presented great opportunities to refine my thinking about leadership in the human service field and to review and incorporate relevant works from other thinkers.

In 2001, I joined the Society for Organizational Learning (SoL), a membership organization founded by Peter Senge, author of *The Fifth Discipline* and other notable books. I became active in SoL and continued to incorporate the most updated thinking and writing on leadership into my work with people with disabilities, their families, and their allies. Since 1996 I have consulted extensively in the areas of leadership and organizational development. Much of what I have learned is included in this book.

Examples are drawn from the lives of real people such as yourself, some of whose names have been changed to protect their privacy. The first four chapters lay the foundation of my approach to leadership by addressing such topics as: Why lead?, What is leadership?, What activates leadership?, and What do leaders do? I recommend that you read straight through these chapters in order to familiarize yourself with my approach. Chapter 5 answers common questions raised by people I've taught and coached; you may have similar questions. Feel free to read this chapter anytime. Chapters 6 through 12 explore core leadership practices in depth. You may want to read these as you run into particular challenges.

Throughout the book, I have included numerous exercises for reflection and self-discovery. If you're like me, sometimes you'll want to stop and do the exercises right away; other times you may be more interested in continuing to read. Feel free to do whatever works best for you. This book is meant to be a resource for you, and I'm sure you know how to make the best use of it.

CHAPTER 1
TOWARD A DEFINITION OF LEADERSHIP

WHY DOES A DEFINITION OF LEADERSHIP MATTER?

You might be tempted to skip over this chapter, thinking, "I'm most interested in how to be a leader, not in a definition of leadership." Many action-oriented people are eager to get moving. They don't necessarily see the value of definitions. But in fact, definitions do matter. Here are some reasons why.

How you define leadership will affect who you think of as a leader. For example, if your definition of leadership focuses on individuals and doesn't allow for the possibility that leadership can be exercised collectively, you might not even notice group leadership when it's occurring. If your definition of leadership strongly includes decisiveness and a "take charge" quality, then that is the kind of person you are likely to align yourself with.

How you define leadership will have an impact on whether you see yourself as a leader. In our culture, the leader as hero is a very prevalent image, resulting in a definition of leadership with strong elements of "command and control." If you are a quiet, laid-back individual who believes leadership is defined as "taking charge," you might fail to envision yourself as a leader at all.

Finally, how you define leadership will play a big role in your evaluation of the quality of your own leadership and that of others. If you envision the leader's role as someone who knows the answers, then you might regularly perceive your own leadership to fall short if you are much more skillful at raising questions than having the answers. In fact, people often feel that it is unacceptable for them to raise a question about why things are the way they are without already having the answers. This is an instance when perfectly

1

valid leadership actions can be impeded by a definition of leadership as "knowing the answers."

To whom do you look for leadership?

The answer to this question is an important clue to your definition of leadership, even if you have never consciously considered what leadership is. Take a minute to jot down the names of three people to whom you look for leadership or have done so in the past. These are not necessarily people whom others would identify as leaders or who have formal positions or titles; they are people you would seek out when confronted with a perplexing challenge or situation that you cannot get clearly sorted out. Later on, we will explore what qualities attract you to these people and use that information in formulating your own personal leadership definition.

One person to whom I have looked for leadership at points in my life is Michael Kendrick. Michael is a longtime international consultant in the disability field. I worked for him in the early to mid-1980s. Later, we worked in overlapping arenas. When I first met him, I was young and extremely opinionated. But because much of my work at the time involved developing new programs with few existing models, I could not always rely on my own knowledge or experience base. Michael afforded a broader perspective on situations in which I was deeply immersed. He would often exhort me not to take things so personally, helping me to analyze a situation systemically. I still draw upon what I learned from him.

More recently, I have benefited from the leadership of people like Peter Senge, author of *The Fifth Discipline,* whose work has contributed enormously to my repertoire. When I was first influenced by Senge, it was completely through his writing; you don't always need to know someone personally to turn to them for leadership.

When asked "To whom do you look for leadership?," people have mentioned spouses, parents, pastors, and teachers. One man, in response to the question *Where have you seen examples of leadership in your life?,* responded, "I would not know where to begin. We see leadership whenever two or more people come together."

To whom do *you* look for leadership? Take a minute to reflect, and then write down the names of several people who come to mind.

WHAT ACTIONS AND PERSONAL QUALITIES CHARACTERIZE THEIR LEADERSHIP?

Once you have several people in mind, ask yourself, "What do these people *do* that makes them a leader? This may be a bit harder to answer, because you will now be digging deeper and surfacing your own assumptions about what constitutes leadership: Do they make sure everyone's voice is heard? Get people focused on the same goal? Convey a sense of confidence and calm that settles people down? Listen well?

When I did this exercise myself, I came up with a core group of practices that seem to be important for people to exercise leadership in the way I define it. Later in the book, I will describe these in more detail. This list was generated by observing the actions of many people whose leadership I admire and trying to determine the common elements. Take a minute to answer the question yourself: What actions and personal qualities characterize the leadership of the people I identified?

WHAT IS YOUR OPERATING DEFINITION OF LEADERSHIP?

Now that you have identified people you consider leaders and explored why you believe that, it's time to create an operating definition of leadership. In other words, how will you know it when you see it?

Here's the challenge: Come up with a one- or two-sentence definition of leadership starting with the phrase, "Leadership is ..." Make sure you define *leadership*, rather than simply listing a collection of personal qualities desirable for a leader. If you have trouble creating a definition, start by incorporating some of the following words:

Art	Generate	Poetry
Fun	Grow	Induce
Joy	Music	Head
Future	Reach	Direct
Pull	Challenge	Walk
Push	New	Results
Power	Win	
Influence	Make	

With groups, I sometimes ask them to create a poster depicting their definition of leadership. If you're feeling especially creative, try doing that. It can make your ideas more tangible. For example, one group created the image of a boat sailing toward the North Star with everyone on board carrying out his/her own particular set of activities: adjusting the sail, preparing food, navigating, and so on. Another group drew a pair of binoculars, aimed at a distant mountain.

A DEFINITION OF LEADERSHIP

Now that you've developed your own definition, it's time to consider mine. I have deliberately waited until this point, because thinking through your own definition helps you to be more conscious of the assumptions that are packed into the word *leadership*. By "assumption" I mean beliefs that are intertwined with your understanding of what leadership is, but which are often unconscious and unarticulated. For example, here are some considerations that are frequently intertwined with the word *leadership*:

- The personal traits or characteristics that count as qualifications for leadership
- The contexts in which leaders might be found, such as occupying formal positions, leading grassroots activities, etc.
- The "unit" of leadership, such as the individual or group (As mentioned earlier, we often think of leadership as solely an individual activity and may therefore fail to notice when it's happening collectively.)
- The relationship between leadership and morality
- A person's actions: that is, the work he or she engages in

The more we reflect on our assumptions about leadership, the more clearly we can separate out these various aspects. For example, what do you think of when someone says, "She's a good leader"? Do you first think about the person's skillfulness, effectiveness, or ability to get the job done? Or do you think about the person's integrity or commitment to a laudable cause? Many people, when referring to a "good leader," not only mean someone who is skillful, but also someone who stands for something they believe in. In fact, the leadership actions a person takes are very much intertwined with their skill as well as both the means they use and the ends they work toward. All three of those can be examined separately, and yet they tend to be lumped together in one word: *leadership*.

Here is my definition: *Leadership is the activity of mobilizing people to work toward a desired future that not only meets people's needs but elevates*

4

them. In order to clarify this definition and to make my assumptions clear, I'd like to break the definition down into several key phrases.

"LEADERSHIP IS THE ACTIVITY ..."

There are numerous definitions of leadership among the thousands of books and articles written on the topic. If you go to the management section of any bookstore, you may be overwhelmed by the number of books that have "leader" or "leadership" in their title. Many definitions of leadership focus on the "leader" as an individual and on the personal qualities that he/she is seen as possessing. I find it more helpful to focus on "leadership" as an activity that can be engaged in by different kinds of people in different roles, not only by people with formal status, title, or position. There are a couple of reasons why I find it more helpful to view leadership this way.

First, it's a more accurate depiction of what actually occurs. There are many kinds of leadership exercised on a day-to-day basis; virtually all leadership involves a network of people working together, either deliberately or coincidentally. People often slip in and out of identified leadership roles, depending on the situation or context. There is also slow, sustained leadership over time, where the individual actions of potentially thousands of people combine to constitute the work of leadership. Think of any social movement. While many of us can identify Martin Luther King Jr. as a key leader of the civil rights movement, do you know the names of any of the other critical leaders during the peak years of that movement? There were hundreds of individuals who played significant roles, and though many of us have never heard of them, we are well aware of the result of that collective activity that we call a movement.

Another example of collective leadership that might be closer to home is a pair of mothers with disabled children. These women exercise leadership aimed at improving care in their local hospital using the "good cop, bad cop" approach. One of them usually takes the role of the demanding, "unreasonable" advocate for the needs of children with significant medical issues; the other acts very cooperative and reasonable. Together they operate as a team. Depending on the activity in which they are engaged, one or the other will take the lead. By focusing on the activity rather than on the individual, many effective leadership combinations can be created.

Another reason why I prefer to focus on leadership as an activity is that people who are relatively new to leadership roles can become discouraged when too much attention is placed on personal qualities or traits. We often start our leadership journey feeling tentative and unsure of ourselves, caring deeply about a person or a cause but not at all confident in our ability (or even desire) to make a difference. This tentativeness will mean we're less inclined to step forward, even on issues that matter to us. Our inner dialogue might go like this: "Who, me? A leader? You must be kidding!" And yet many people take on leadership roles, not because they want to be a leader, but because they feel called to exercise leadership toward something they care about. If they had the choice, they'd rather let someone else do it. Any model of leadership that creates obstacles to stepping forward toward addressing a situation that one cares about is problematic.

As Peter Block writes, "The belief that the power lies 'up there' is a way of ensuring our own helplessness, all for the relief of an imagined moment of safety."[1] This "imagined moment of safety" is our fantasy that someone else "up there" or "out there" is better qualified to take action on matters that we care about. Focusing on leadership as an activity puts the emphasis where it should be—on the work we need to engage in to bring about our vision. It opens up all sorts of possibilities for how the work might be organized. It doesn't preclude actions by individuals, but it allows for shared leadership, leadership over long periods of time, rotating leadership, imperfect leadership, and so on. Also, a focus on leadership as an activity or journey is more forgiving. You can take some steps, learn from them, and try again ... rather than feeling like you have to get it perfect all the time.

"MOBILIZING PEOPLE TO WORK TOWARD A DESIRED FUTURE ..."

The second key aspect of this definition relates to the nature of the activity. The implication of this phrase is that leadership is about movement, change, and growth, which bridge the gap between our current state and our desired future. Implicit in the phrase is the assumption that leadership is needed when things are not the way we want them to be. Later in the book, we'll talk more about exactly what leaders do to facilitate that movement, because that is truly the work of leadership.

When we talk about "desired future" we introduce the concept of vision, of something to strive toward. Geoffrey Bellman writes, "Leadership can be seen as energy collected, directed, and released toward a future vision."[2] He makes the point that before a person decides to follow someone, that person has already made a commitment to a vision, a desired future. This is the activator of their leadership journey, something we'll explore more fully in the next chapter.

There's a quote in the Bible that says, "Where there is no vision, the people perish" (Proverbs 29:18). Having a vision to move toward is life-enhancing; it generates energy and momentum. The quote is a great reminder of the potency of vision in a metaphorical way. Yet it is not just a figure of speech; it is literally true. If our vision excludes certain voices, people, or perspectives, then you can be sure that they will not be present.

For example, there was once a newspaper article about children with developmental disabilities in Russia. This was not that long ago, yet many of these children were locked up in archaic facilities termed by one man as "little gulags." The article went on to say that the children were locked up because of a widespread belief that they were subhuman, and that Soviet thinking has been oriented toward a perfect future and a perfect individual; therefore, people who were not perfect were considered subhuman. You can see in this example, which stands for many similar examples, that a vision that excludes certain people will make sure they are not present. That's the power of vision.

On an individual level, if our vision for specific people isn't colorful, vital, and clear, how will we find the energy to help them work toward such a life? How will we convince others to do so? How will we sustain ourselves during the tough times? Having a vision is extremely important yet challenging, and I will address it in more detail soon.

"THAT NOT ONLY MEETS PEOPLE'S NEEDS BUT ELEVATES THEM ..."

Here is the final phrase in my leadership definition, a phrase I borrowed from James McGregor Burns. This is the moral component to the definition, the part that says just having a vision isn't enough; it needs to be a vision that is transcendent, that contributes to the greater good. Hitler had a vision: it was sharp and colorful and convincing to many, many people. Millions of people died as a result of his vision. While it is important to have a vision, the content of that vision is just as important.

Although I stop short of offering a prescription for the content of your personal vision, I do believe there are certain principles that contribute to the aspiration of not only meeting people's needs but elevating them.

- Working toward this vision brings out the good in people.
- People are inclined to act with compassion toward even the most disadvantaged members.
- The vision equalizes and even elevates the status of people who are generally disregarded or overlooked.
- The vision promotes life and a rich quality of life vs. death and a diminished quality of life.

7

- People are encouraged to live the Golden Rule, or the ethic of reciprocity, which is found in the scriptures of nearly every religion.

One Christian version of the Golden Rule that I grew up with is "Love your neighbor as yourself."[3] Take a minute to think about the definition of leadership I've presented and how it compares to yours. Are there important aspects of your definition that are not addressed in mine? Are there some elements of mine that stimulate you to think differently about your conception of leadership?

In this chapter, I have tried to demonstrate that having a working definition of leadership helps to shape the way you perceive and evaluate your own actions and those of others. I have encouraged you to develop your own definition of leadership, one that fits your experience and role models. I have shared my working definition of leadership, which was developed in much the same way that I asked you to create your own. In the next chapter, we will address the question of motivation: why would one want to exercise leadership, and what are some equally compelling reasons not to lead?

Chapter 2
Motivation: The Leadership Activator

The movement toward leadership

Leadership is a journey that begins with a decision to act. It is an internal shift that results in external action. From a position of passively accepting events that unfold on their own, you move to actively exerting influence over the events at hand. Initially, you may feel very tentative and unsure. Perhaps you compare yourself unfavorably to your role models, people who have made a difference in the social service field, or politicians or religious figures. Whoever they are, you see these role models as more advanced or capable than you; you doubt you have anything to offer in the leadership arena. Or perhaps it is just not in your personality to be proactive. You'd rather wait for someone else to take the lead, and then you are perfectly willing to help out. Maybe up until now you've sat back and waited for others to take action, complaining, perhaps, about your powerlessness. But then something happens and, in spite of your doubts, you find yourself taking that step.

There are a variety of circumstances that contribute to the movement toward leadership. Perhaps you have supported others whose leadership has not been effective. After giving them the benefit of the doubt, you realize that not only is nothing positive happening, but you could (possibly) do a better job. So you decide to step forward. Or maybe you are frustrated that no one seems to be exercising leadership. Over time, your frustration becomes a stronger force than your hesitation. Maybe you've had the unfortunate experience of affiliating yourself with people whose leadership turned out to be in pursuit of ends you don't support. As a result, you decide it's time for you to move into a more active leadership role on behalf of issues you do support. It's also possible that, like me, you were recruited into a leadership role rather than volunteering.

In the late 1970s, I was approached by a manager with the local office of the state Department of Mental Retardation. He asked whether I would be interested in creating a new residential agency that would serve four teenaged girls with multiple disabilities who were living at a nearby institution, Belchertown State School. The state had put out requests for proposals several times, and none of the existing community service providers had bid on the contract.

Although I had worked with people with developmental disabilities for several years, I had virtually no management or leadership experience. I was only twenty-four years old. To this day, I cannot say with certainty what motivated me to accept the challenge. I know I was caught up in the excitement of the times: deinstitutionalization was in full swing, and the community service system was rapidly expanding. There was a sense of mission, righteousness, and solidarity among the proponents of deinstitutionalization. On a practical level, the state manager promised extensive support from his office while I was developing the skills I needed to create and manage an agency.

But no previous experiences had prepared me to form a nonprofit corporation, purchase and renovate a residence so it would be wheelchair accessible, develop policies and procedures, hire and supervise staff, set up and manage the agency's finances, or ensure that we provided high quality services to the young women. If I had truly known what was involved, I probably would not have accepted the challenge. And yet, having worked at Belchertown State School while in college, I had a serious commitment to helping people move out of institutions and create their own homes in the community. In spite of deep reservations about my preparedness for the role, I felt a strong motivation to take on the leadership challenge offered to me.

Since that time, I've had numerous opportunities to exercise leadership, formally and informally. In spite of over thirty years of experience and increased confidence in my own capabilities, I still confront new challenges with trepidation. What supports me is my motivation to address a situation or need that has an impact on people's lives.

SOURCES OF MOTIVATION

Virginia (a pseudonym) is another example of someone who didn't go looking for a leadership role. Although many professionals and family members identify her as a role model, she doesn't think of herself that way. Over the years, Virginia, the mother of a daughter with disabilities, has taken on increasingly senior leadership roles in her state. She founded a local family leadership organization along with a leadership training series. In addition, she was a founder of the statewide family organization that shepherded the passage of legislation requiring agencies serving people with disabilities to consult with families to coordinate support services for their clients. This legislation, informally called the Family Support Bill, took eleven years to pass and required unceasing advocacy to bring it to fruition.

Virginia is a top leader of an agency serving people with developmental disabilities. In spite of these numerous leadership roles, when I asked Virginia what led her to become a leader, she said, "You find yourself in various roles that other people would say are leadership when you are motivated by something that's very personal. It's all about my daughter. How could I do any less? If it moves from helping her to something that helps other people, that's an accident. It's not what I would have chosen. I'd rather be in my garden or baking every single day. But I can't fulfill my role as her mother in any other way than what I'm doing. I have a tremendous desire to see the world change for all people with disabilities, because my daughter is always in jeopardy. If other people are not in a good situation, it's harder for her to have a good life." Virginia's motivation to act on behalf of her daughter provides her with a sense of urgency: mediocre is insufficient; tomorrow is too late.

Many other family members, as well as people with disabilities and their allies, share Virginia's perspective on leadership. They did not take on leadership roles because of an inner drive to lead. Instead, external circumstances reached into them, connected with a deep source of motivation, and pulled them forward. The story of Rosa Parks, the woman who became a powerful symbol during the civil rights movement, is a good example of this dynamic. You may recall that she was a middle-aged seamstress on her way home from work in Montgomery, Alabama, on December 1, 1955. Ms. Parks decided to do something that was both illegal and culturally unacceptable in that racist society—and was also very dangerous: she sat down in the front of a bus in a seat reserved for whites. The story is often told that she sat down because she was "tired." Yes, that is what she told others when asked what her motivation to act had been. However, the full meaning of "tired" needs further explanation.

You see, Rosa Parks was not just a middle-aged seamstress. She was also well trained in the theory and tactics of nonviolence and had studied in the company of Martin Luther King Jr. She was secretary of the Montgomery chapter of the NAACP, where they had also discussed nonviolence. Ms. Parks' "tiredness" was not only physical, it was also spiritual. In the words of Parker Palmer, she was "tired in her heart and

11

in her soul, tired not only of racism but of her own complicity in the diminishing effects of racism ..."[24] In other words, external circumstances reached into her and took hold of a deep source of motivation. In her case, as Palmer asserts, she wished to live a life "divided no more."

Based on this understanding, I want to put forward a fundamental point of this book. Wherever you are on your leadership journey, motivation is the central element. It is the stimulus, the activator of leadership. It's the switch that enables you to make the internal shift described above, the start of your leadership journey. Once you begin that journey, the necessary skills can be acquired, borrowed, or shared. Although personal traits such as organization and charisma are useful in the exercise of leadership, they are not central. What can't be borrowed, at least initially, is motivation. You really need to have a strong reason to take that first step.

Let's start by looking at the word *motivation*. Take a minute to think about how you would define it. Is it willpower—the act of mentally toughening yourself to act in ways that do not come naturally? Or is it passion—that strong energy that wipes away all impediments? Motivation, defined as "drive" or "incentive," will be experienced differently by different people. But its core function is the same: to get you moving. It's the fuel, the juice, the energy that gets you started and sustains you. And I guarantee that you can have all the potential in the world to be a leader but if you lack motivation you will never get out of the starting gate.

There are two fundamental sources of motivation to lead. The first is what I would characterize as *constitutional motivation*. This applies to people with an inner urge to lead; they are driven to exercise leadership and would do so in virtually any context. For example, there is an experiential exercise that I use in some of my leadership courses called Evacuation Drill. Its premise is that the group is faced with an imminent threat and needs to evacuate their current location immediately. The group is charged with the task of planning a move to a remote location for an indeterminate length of time. They have ten minutes to plan their evacuation; each person is allowed to bring one item from their current location that they believe to be essential to their survival. The group must then plan their trip. The point of this exercise is to examine how people organize themselves to accomplish a task when they are under stress, and to explore the leadership patterns that emerge.

Inevitably, one or two people immediately step forward and begin to organize the rest of the group. Initially, other members of the group gravitate toward those individuals, no matter what they propose. As additional proposals are made, a plan begins to take shape. The people who initially step forward are often these constitutional leaders, individuals who have the inner drive to lead whenever there is a void. However, along with the constitutional motivation to lead, there are other motivations as well. In the Evacuation Drill exercise, there are individuals whose voices emerge gradually, perhaps motivated by a strong sense of what's right or by concern for the well-being of the group. These voices blend with those of others and can play a pivotal role in determining the course of action. While their leadership is usually more subtle, it still has a decisive impact.

The second source of motivation is what I would characterize as *situational motivation*. For example, some people—and many family members and people with disabilities fall into this category—take on leadership roles because they are directly affected by the issues at stake. There is something about their situation or that of a family member that needs to be improved. It's very possible that they would never have become a leader without that source of motivation, as Virginia acknowledged. I call these people "reluctant leaders." One mother of a child with disabilities told a group of other family members that she had no interest in exercising leadership until well after her child was born. She said, "My husband and I were on a career track. We wanted to have it all: good jobs, a beautiful home, nice cars. Even after Andrew was born, I held on to that dream. But at some point I realized that if he was going to have a decent life, and if we were going to do okay as a family, I had to put that energy into advocating for him instead of acquiring more possessions. It was hard to change gears, but I had no choice."

People motivated to exercise leadership by external circumstances initially may not think of themselves as leaders. For example, at first this mother did not think of her actions on behalf of her son as leadership. Instead, she saw herself as just doing what needed to be done. In her mind, leadership was something dramatic and decisive, a kind of command-and-control approach that had been shaped by her experience as a manager in a hierarchical company. Over time, as a result of taking part in leadership training and being mentored by other parent leaders, she began to see her actions as leadership. This transition is common to many people who exercise leadership reluctantly. At some point in their journey, such people go from "just doing what needs to be done" to making a commitment to exercise leadership. Such a commitment does not need to be an intellectual one. Sometimes a commitment of the heart is made before the mind even knows it.

In addition to those people motivated to exercise leadership because circumstances directly affect them, there are also people motivated to exercise leadership because they *identify* with those who are directly affected. Perhaps they have heard compelling stories of injustice or have

13

known people who experienced discrimination. Such people may feel a sense of interconnectedness with others and be moved to take leadership out of a sense of compassion. Many allies of people with disabilities and their families are motivated in this way. Sometimes this is viewed by those directly affected as suspect or inauthentic. After all, why would anyone who didn't have to address these issues do so voluntarily?

I once had to defend my commitment to supporting people with psychiatric disabilities to have a voice, having been challenged by one of the leaders in the psychiatric survivors' movement. He questioned my motivation and my authenticity. Although it was painful at the time, it compelled me to clearly articulate my own personal stake and point of identification with the people I was working for. This, in turn, strengthened my own motivation, because I realized that I was as personally affected as if it were my own voice that was being suppressed—and that it could well be my voice in another context.

In his book *The Longing for Home,* Frederick Buechner speaks to this motivation: "We carry inside us a vision of wholeness that we sense is our true home ... But woe to us if we forget the homeless ones who have no vote, no power, nobody to lobby for them, who might as well have no faces ... To be really at home is to be really at peace and our lives so intrinsically interwoven that there can be no peace for any of us until there is real peace for all of us."[5]

Just as I was writing about this source of motivation, my friend and colleague Karlene called. She is a paragon of compassion. She spends her life working on behalf of others: driving people to church, working in a human service agency, serving on a myriad of committees, teaching classes. In addition to her unstinting service, she has also played many leadership roles. She was moderator at her church for a number of years, she serves on multiple nonprofit boards, and she has initiated several projects that promote the integration of people with disabilities into their communities. When I asked her why she was motivated to exercise leadership, she replied, "I don't even see it as leadership. It's a natural reaction that comes from an underlying desire to be helpful. I meet a person, and right away I know someone else who could be helpful to them ... I have gotten to personally know so many people with disabilities and I have seen firsthand how their lives can get so much better with a little help from others." For Karlene, exercising leadership satisfies her deep desire to be helpful.

What are *your* sources of motivation? It's time to begin identifying the inner and outer fuel for your own leadership journey. Whether you are a person just starting on the path or someone who is well-seasoned, there are things that attract and sustain you. Spend a minute reflecting on these questions:

1. Why exercise leadership?
2. Why *not* exercise leadership?
3. Of the above, which are the most powerful reasons—for me—in favor of leading?
4. Of the above, which are the most powerful reasons—for me—against leading?

You might also want to spend some time talking with family members, friends, and colleagues about your answers to these questions, as the people in your life offer useful perspectives on your sources of motivation.

I have asked these questions at leadership workshops for families of people with disabilities. We usually begin by identifying some of the reasons *not* to lead, of which there are many. Sometimes the reasons not to lead can seem stronger and more compelling than the reasons *to* lead. When you reflect on all the possible obstacles to leadership, the importance of motivation becomes even clearer.

REASONS NOT TO LEAD

Self-doubt is perhaps the biggest impediment to leadership. The prospect of exercising leadership can be intimidating, scary, and anxiety-provoking. People often fear being unfavorably held up against a set of personal characteristics they believe are prerequisites for leadership, even if they have never consciously thought it through. Because of this self-doubt, leadership may be viewed as someone else's role—perhaps someone decisive, charismatic, and organized. Self-doubt can be a powerful impediment to the exercise of leadership when it creates a self-fulfilling prophecy. If someone doubts himself to the point where he fails to exercise leadership, then he will not gain the necessary experience that might increase his confidence.

At one leadership event, a participant asked how she might develop the confidence to exercise leadership. She said she had often taken one step forward, then questioned herself and taken two steps back. She described a pattern of acting with conviction in response to a compelling need, then becoming frozen with self-doubt about the action she had taken and consequently undoing her first confident action. We talked about what was causing her to question herself and discovered that it came from her belief that there was a "right way" to act that was unknown to her. We also

15

talked about the fact that her backtracking was causing more harm than moving forward imperfectly would have. In response to her question about developing confidence, my best advice was, "Fake your confidence, keep moving forward, and learn from your actions."

A variation on the theme of self-doubt is the belief that leaders have to know the answers in order to lead. The leadership job description that many of us of carry around in our heads includes "knowing the answers" as one important duty. As we will discuss later, "knowing the answers" is not a leadership requirement, and it may actually prevent one from acting as skillfully as possible by enabling others to avoid taking responsibility, suppressing creative thinking, and keeping others at a distance. However, because we often think of leaders as the people with the answers, we can fail to step forward if we feel we don't have the answers.

Believing that leadership can (or should) only be exercised by someone with a formal position or title is another perceived reason not to lead. Like the reasons described above, this perception works against the development of capabilities and experiences that contribute to a person becoming an effective leader, whether they have a title or not. It also places responsibility and power in the hands of another party. All three of these reasons spring from one common cause: a set of assumptions (our unconscious job description) about the skills, duties, and prerequisites for being a leader. Later in this book, we will examine your assumptions in more detail.

Speaking of assumptions, another reason not to lead is the belief that no intervention can impact on the course of events. Our taken-for-granted beliefs about how change occurs play a significant role in determining whether we try to influence what is happening around us. If we believe that events are predetermined, then we may be inclined to play a passive role. Sometimes, passivity is the result of self-doubt, but it can also come from a deeper set of beliefs about how the world operates. For example, you might believe that the past determines the future. Psychologist Martin Seligman writes, "Do you believe your past determines your future? This is not an idle question of philosophical theory. To the extent that you believe that the past determines the future, you will tend to allow yourself to be a passive vessel that does not actively change its course. Such beliefs are responsible for magnifying many people's inertia."[6] Any beliefs that minimize the potential for humans to influence events is likely to be an impediment to the exercise of leadership.

Another reason not to lead is an array of overwhelming responsibilities: caring for a child who has a disability, trying to advocate for quality education, tending to the needs of other family members, holding down a job. Often, one's own individual situation is challenging enough, without taking on broader leadership roles. One mother, Diane, talked about how she had gone from viewing her family's situation as their own individual responsibility to realizing that, if families joined together, they could positively influence the circumstances of the whole. She described that realization as the beginning of her leadership journey.

But there are points in everyone's life when the prospect of taking on broader responsibilities is just impossible to imagine. During those times, it might be comforting to remember that even when you are caring for one person, you can practice the work of leadership. That's another of those misperceptions that gets in the way of exercising leadership: that it has to be on a large scale to be considered leadership. One mother of two children with autism told the story of how her son had been treated disrespectfully by the gym teacher at his school. Her response? To advocate that training on autism be conducted with all the school personnel. Not only was the intervention designed to address her son's individual situation, but it had the added benefit of affecting all the students with autism who attended that school.

Lack of support, cooperation, or appreciation are also reasons why people avoid taking on leadership roles. One parent talked about her efforts to start a Parent Advisory Council for her school system. She spent an entire year trying to recruit families to attend monthly meetings. Every month, the same small group showed up. When they sent out surveys, the surveys came back with great suggestions and encouragement for the PAC to continue and even grow. However, few people were willing to help out. We did an analysis of what this parent had done to recruit a wider array of people to play active roles within the PAC and came up with a plan for the next year. Shortly after that, she told me she had resigned from her leadership position because she was tired of the lack of support. This is not an uncommon situation in volunteer efforts, and it can be a very strong reason why people refuse to take leadership.

Some people are uncomfortable with the prospect of separating themselves from the group in order to assume a leadership role. They describe the experience as lonely. Although exercising leadership can involve leaving the safety of the group and distinguishing oneself, it's often the stories we tell ourselves about how leaders need to behave that cause this concern. When we carry the notion that a leader always goes *before* rather than *with* her people, our fears of isolation and loneliness can be magnified. On the other hand, if you cannot bear to set yourself apart from the group, then perhaps responsible follower-ship, not leadership, is an appropriate role for you.

Another reason not to lead is the fear of losing what you have, whether it is income, status, security, or relationship. This is a compelling reason to seriously consider whether you want to assume a leadership role: the risks are real. As Heifetz and Linsky write, "It is no wonder that when the myriad opportunities to exercise leadership call, you often hesitate. Anyone who has stepped out on the line, leading part or all of an organization, a community, or a family knows the personal and professional vulnerabilities. However gentle your style, however careful your strategy, however sure you may be that you are on the right track, leading is risky."[7] And yet these authors encourage people to take leadership, stating, "… We believe that leadership, while perilous, is an enterprise worthy of the costs."[8]

Fear of change is yet another reason not to take leadership. "Change" in this context can be internal or external. Assuming leadership when one has not previously done so involves changes in oneself—speaking out when one has hung back, acting assertively even when one feels hesitant, paying attention to the perspectives of the whole group rather than just one's own point of view, distancing oneself somewhat from your former peers. And assuming leadership usually results in changes in the situation being addressed—or at least one intends that to happen. Almost by definition, leadership involves being in the midst of change, whether you are promoting or opposing it. People who have issues with change—inside or outside themselves—may be reluctant to step into leadership roles.

These are some of the major reasons not to lead. Perhaps you have thought of others that are specific to you. Given all the factors working against leadership, why would anyone want to become a leader?

REASONS TO LEAD

Probably the strongest reason to lead is that you feel a need and it is not being addressed. You see a situation that needs changing, whether it is in the life of one person or on a larger scale. A situation or need calling for leadership is probably the strongest motivator there is, especially if it's something you care deeply about.

There is an excellent exercise from a time-management program I discovered years ago. Called the "I-beam exercise," it asks you to imagine you are at the top of a tall skyscraper. Across the way is another tall skyscraper. There is an I-beam (a narrow steel beam) suspended between the two. The facilitator asks, "Would you walk across this I-beam for $10?" The participants usually respond, "No way!"

"How about for $100? $1000? $1,000,000?" He then raises the stakes by asking you to imagine that it is sleeting, and the wind is blowing. "What would cause you to walk across this I-beam?" Usually the answer is someone or something that the person cares deeply about. This is the most powerful motivator. If you think of your leadership journey as a walk across that I-beam, then a situation or need that motivates you is your strongest reason to lead. In fact, later is this book, we will focus on clearly identifying a situation or need that motivates you.

In my experience, it is very difficult to engage someone in a sustained commitment to anything unless there is a deep, heartfelt aspect to a person's motivation. It can't be at an intellectual level alone. Years ago I organized a conference entitled, "Personal Commitment and Social Change." I clearly remember one interaction during the conference that crystallized this point. Philip Berrigan, well-known nuclear disarmament activist, had just finished a keynote presentation that compellingly described how he had been drawn to that issue. Psychiatric rights activist, Judi Chamberlin, stood up and challenged Berrigan to extend his commitment to people with psychiatric disabilities. Berrigan responded, not unreasonably, that if the world continued on its present path toward nuclear war, there would not *be* any people with psychiatric disabilities to advocate for. Chamberlin, unsatisfied with his logic, pressed her point. A standoff ensued. I was left feeling profoundly grateful that these two strong leaders had each made a commitment to a cause that was compelling to them, yet I was puzzled by their inability to recognize that each had a particular calling. It was clear that neither was going to recruit the other to their cause, even if it made sense logically.

There are ancillary benefits to exercising leadership: to learn, to feel solidarity with others on the journey, to experience a sense of accomplishment, to teach others, to leave a legacy. These reasons are especially powerful motivators when they coincide with a compelling situation or need. If you find yourself in leadership roles that feel hollow or unsatisfying, it may be that you are getting some of these ancillary benefits without the added potency of being connected to a situation that engages you at a deep level. An overdeveloped sense of responsibility or duty can land you in such circumstances. There are far more compelling needs than there are leaders. Out of a sense of responsibility, we can find ourselves recruited to causes that do not resonate. This is not necessarily a bad thing but you will have far more potency and sustainability if you are aligned with a situation that resonates.

Motivation is not a once-and-for-all thing. It waxes and wanes by the day, depending on how you feel physically and emotionally. If you are going through a wrenching time personally, it's going to be challenging for you to stay motivated to run an advocacy group. That's natural. But motivation is like a touchstone: it's something you can go back to when you feel depleted or begin to question why you ever made the commitment to lead. The day I interviewed Virginia, she talked about how she felt overwhelmed and exhausted. She was worried about how she was going to gracefully fulfill the many commitments she had made. We talked for a long time about what was her deepest source of motivation—her daughter—and how she might arrange her schedule to spend more time with her. In the midst of a schedule so full of commitments that it was hard to come up for air, Virginia had accidentally lost her touchstone, her abiding source of motivation.

Maybe it is even helpful to have some kind of physical symbol of your motivation that you can see and feel when you are in that questioning mode. During the writing of this book, I taped up a photograph of a group of families with whom I regularly work. They encouraged me during my search for a publisher and gave me confidence that I had an interested audience by affirming the usefulness of what I have to share. Their stories are a powerful motivator and the photograph reminds me of those stories. Whenever I lose momentum, I look at the picture and it reenergizes me.

Motivation also rubs off. Initially you may feel pretty lonely in your resolve, but as you move forward, you engage the motivation of others, which strengthens your own. Feeling responsible to and for other people is a powerful source of motivation. We create a web of responsibility that keeps us moving, even when we'd really like to drop the ball. Scholar and consultant William Isaacs shared some of the lessons he'd learned from the civil rights movement, particularly about large-scale change. He commented on how momentum was created: it started small, with as few as two people, and a sense of resonance with others. He stated, "Two makes an aperture, a microcosm of a shift." The creation of momentum through the joining together of small groups is the hallmark of any social movement; one can think of each person's motivation as being multiplied exponentially as they join together with others.

Our motivation can be especially strengthened if we feel we have a singular contribution to make, that there will be a void if we fail to show up. There is a wonderful story told by a colleague about a gentleman with developmental disabilities who was a member of the choir at his church. He received notification that he had won an award from a citizens' group affiliated with the Department of Mental Retardation. He declined to attend the awards ceremony because it conflicted with choir practice. Upon hearing that, an official with the Department personally called the gentleman and pleaded with him to attend. Politely but firmly, this man again declined, stating that he needed to be present at choir practice because "they need my voice." Even during those times when our motivation is put to the test, knowing that others need our voice can keep us engaged.

Once you start seeing the fruits of your leadership—motivation made manifest—your resolve is often strengthened. Those tentative first few steps in the direction of your aspiration become more and more confident. In the next chapter, we will focus on the task of identifying your aspiration. What are the purposes or aims of your leadership? Such clarity can help focus your efforts enormously and attract others to the effort.

CHAPTER 3
LEADERSHIP TOWARD WHAT?
CREATING A VISION OF POSSIBILITY

THE POWER OF VISION

The poet Rainer Maria Rilke wrote this evocative passage:

> "You must give birth to your images.
> They are the future waiting to be born.
> Fear not the strangeness you feel.
> The future must enter you
> long before it happens.
> Just wait for the birth,
> for the hour of new clarity."[9]

Many people who are trying to give birth to their images do indeed feel strange. There's a sense of something ahead, but initially it can be hazy and unclear. And how to get there is often a complete mystery. There can be self-doubt, especially if others are raising questions. At this point, learning to trust oneself, finding ways to crystallize that vision, and then figuring out how to move toward the vision and bring others along are critical elements of this part of the leadership journey.

Some years ago, I discovered Appreciative Inquiry, an approach to organization and community change that aids people to create a clear and compelling vision of the future. Appreciative Inquiry is a form of action research developed by David Cooperrider and colleagues in the late 1980s. Drawing from evidence in at least half a dozen fields and based on research in over one hundred countries, Appreciative Inquiry is "a form of transformational inquiry that selectively seeks to locate, highlight, and illuminate the 'life-giving' forces of an organization's existence."[10]

Sue Hammond captures the power of Appreciative Inquiry as a way to create organizational change. She states that assumptions, which are shared beliefs that cause a group to think and act in certain ways, often interfere with seeing or discovering other data that may contradict those beliefs and thus result in missed opportunities. The typical approach to change is to identify and diagnose the problem and then try to find a solution. Since the major focus is on problems, it is problems that are found and emphasized.

One of the assumptions of Appreciative Inquiry is that *what we focus on becomes our reality*. "If we focus on what is wrong or what is missing, we tend to see everything through that filter or frame. The filter or frame is our unconscious set of assumptions. We tend not to be aware of our frame, and we fail to notice that we disregard information that doesn't fit our reality ... In order to see data that conflict with our assumptions, we have to break outside of our filter or frame."[11]

A premise of Appreciative Inquiry that I find particularly compelling is the "heliotropic hypothesis." *Heliotropic* means to turn toward the sun, just as sunflowers or rain lilies do. The heliotropic hypothesis states that "human systems have an observable tendency to evolve in the direction of those positive images that are the brightest and boldest, most illuminating and promising"[12] There is research that suggests that when people create a clear and compelling vision, this positively affects what actually happens. For example, imagery techniques are becoming important to the training of successful athletes.

In another arena, the power of positive images has also been established. Scholars have discovered that the underlying images held by a civilization or culture greatly influence its fate. Dutch sociologist Fred Polak, who has studied western civilization, argues that a positive image of the future is the single most important variable for understanding cultural evolution. When a culture holds a positive and dynamic image of the future, it grows toward that image. Once the image begins to decay and lose vitality, the culture does not long survive. Of course, this finding was anticipated by the Proverbs 29:18 biblical quote: "Where there is no vision, the people perish."

Since I first learned about Appreciative Inquiry, I have incorporated this perspective more and more into my professional and personal life. Appreciative Inquiry has been used and proven in numerous fields and across scores of organizations and communities, but that is not the main reason I recommend the adoption of this perspective. The plain fact is, it just makes sense. It does not in any way deny the harmful things occurring in the world. However, it is a conscious choice to discover what is working in a person's life or an organization and to strengthen that rather than put the same amount of effort into fixing what is wrong. Bill Joy, founder and former chief scientist of Sun Microsystems captures this choice: "We have to encourage the future we want rather than trying to prevent the future we fear."[13]

POSITIVE OR NEGATIVE VISION?

Peter Senge writes about the difference between positive and negative vision. He writes, "'What do we want?' is different from 'What do we want to avoid?'"[14] He goes on to observe that although the difference is obvious, negative visions are much more common than positive vision. How often have you had the experience of fighting something bad, whether it was poor quality services, a special education department that was anything but special, or fighting against budget cuts? Didn't you feel a strong sense of camaraderie with your fellow fighters? A feeling that you had a clear focus or target of your energy? When we fight against something negative, we often generate great passion and a focused sense of purpose.

But Senge notes that negative visions have limitations. First, energy that could be invested in creating something new is directed toward preventing something we want to avoid. Ironically, when we focus on what we don't want, we give that more potency and may inadvertently strengthen it! Second, a negative vision, although it might initially be a good catalyst, also has a sense of powerlessness associated with it, kind of a one-down, victim perspective. And third, negative visions can only be sustained as long as the threat persists, so they are inevitably short-lived.

Although initially more challenging to mobilize around, positive visions can be motivating and uplifting, create forward momentum, and serve as a way to bond people in the deepest way possible. And if we believe that "what we focus on becomes our reality" what better place to focus than on a positive vision?

WHAT IS VISION?

Up to this point, we have not really addressed what vision actually is. It's a word in common usage today, but what does it really mean? Derived from the Latin *vidēre*, "to see," the word can be used both as a noun ("something seen; the act or power of seeing") and as a verb ("to make evident to the sight"). I think of vision as an image or picture of the future we are trying to bring into existence, a picture so clear that it can shape day-to-day actions and decisions and pull people forward toward it. A vision is a North Star, something to guide you and keep you oriented in the right direction. At the same time, it needs to be specific enough to help shape your future. Broad abstract statements such as "people will have self-determination" or "people will be respected" may be a good starting point, but they lack the clarity and specificity that can distinguish one person's or group's vision from another. Vision encompasses such things as dreams, wants, hopes, values, aspirations, ideals, principles, and desired future.

Kouzes and Posner[15] describe four attributes of vision: future orientation, clarity of the image, evoking ideals and standards of excellence, and uniqueness. Their definition of vision is "an ideal and unique image of the future."

What might your vision encompass? Any area of your life that is important to you and where you are both able and willing to have an impact. It's up to you to define the arenas where you want to focus but keep in mind that a vision exercise is only productive if you are truly motivated to bring something positive into existence in the areas you choose.

POSSIBLE SOURCES OF VISION

One source of vision, at least as a starting point, is dissatisfaction with current reality. Organizational consultants Dannemiller Tyson have developed a very useful model describing conditions most conducive to a change effort. By "change effort" I mean moving from current reality toward an image or vision of the future in an intentional way. The four conditions in this model are dissatisfaction with the current situation (D), vision of the future that is positive, compelling, and possible (V), first steps in the direction of the vision (F), and resistance to change (R). This model is often stated as an equation: $D + V + F > R$.[16]

The model posits that conditions for change are favorable if the sum of dissatisfaction, vision, and first steps is greater than resistance. If resistance is strong, then one or more of these other factors will need to be strengthened or change will not occur. Dissatisfaction with the current situation is often the initial catalyzing force, a positive precondition to the exercise of leadership. As a colleague once said, "Dissatisfaction is like looking into the abyss; it frightens people and makes them want to take action." But unless you quickly establish a vision of the future that is positive, compelling, and possible, discouragement and a sense of hopelessness are likely to set in. And if there is dissatisfaction combined with a vision of the future but no clarity about first steps, then the gap

25

between the desired future and the current reality may be too great to create the momentum needed to move toward the vision. This formula can be a helpful way to take that critical step to moving toward your vision and shed light on what strategies might facilitate a change. Leaders need to pay close attention to the ongoing interplay between these four conditions.

In my experience, people often create a vision as the result of a current situation that is not up to par, even though they've created a positive vision. Let's say that your dissatisfaction with the loneliness and isolation of many people with disabilities is the catalyst for your vision. That vision might be something like "people with disabilities are appreciated and respected for the contributions they make to others' lives." Even when you start from a place of dissatisfaction, you can create a positive vision. And a positive vision generates energy, enthusiasm, and momentum.

One of my coaching clients came to our meeting feeling down and discouraged. He complained that during the past couple of months we had focused on the things that weren't working for him and how little he could do to change that. He said, "These sessions are starting to get dark and gloomy instead of bright and uplifting," and he attributed that to the fact that we'd been focusing on what was wrong in his life instead of moving forward toward his vision. Once we put our focus back on the vision, his whole mood shifted, and he left the session feeling confident and upbeat.

Another source of vision is the experience of other people. This can be very helpful, since people sometimes lack experiences from which to create their own vision of a positive future. I once worked with a group of government and nonprofit managers from Ukraine. One of the participants, a man who worked with the local government, was very excited about shared living as an alternative to the institutions that housed people with disabilities. Shared living is a model where one person with a disability shares a home with a family or another community member rather than living with a group of other people with disabilities. This gentleman was very eager to go home and implement "shared living," but his vision was that eight or more individuals with disabilities would live with a family! He very much wanted to see the people he served have a better life, but his vision was limited by the conditions he was familiar with. Before creating a vision for yourself, it can be helpful to do some research about what's possible outside of your existing frame of reference.

Another source of vision is intuition. Kouzes and Posner write, "Intuition is the wellspring of vision."[17] But what, in fact, is intuition? Is it a magical, mystical, irrational energy source that only a few people have access to? Not according to cognitive psychologist Gary Klein. For over twenty years, Dr. Klein has studied men and woman who make split-second decisions in high-stakes circumstances to find out how they use intuition to help them make decisions. What he discovered from the firefighters, soldiers, and intensive care professionals he studied is that intuition comes down to two things: *recognition* and *simulation*.

The first step in harnessing intuition to make decisions is "learning how to see—looking for cues or patterns that ultimately show you what to do."[18] This is what Klein means by *recognition*. What this means for the visioning process is that what you envision is not some out-of-the-blue image of an ideal future, but the use of your intuition to put together the little details of what is important and unique about the person or group that you are creating a vision for. For example, if a person is attracted to being outdoors, you might ask yourself: "What clues might there be for a desired future?" Gwen, the mother of an artistically talented young woman with Down syndrome, started seeing those clues when her daughter was young. Although Joy had many interests as a child, she kept coming back over and over to drawing tools. Encouraged by her family to pursue her interest in art, she is now an accomplished artist.

Similarly, Jane, whose daughter Ann has for years taken a week-long cruise with several friends, did not sit down and do a systematic inventory of what experiences were lacking in Ann's life and what could be added. Instead, she thought about Ann and her love of people and partying, and all of a sudden the idea of a cruise came to her.

Once people who use their intuition size up a situation and decide to take action, they use *simulation* to preview the quality of their decision. In other words, they mentally run through various scenarios of what might happen as a result of their decision before taking action. You can use this preview technique to verify whether what you have envisioned is likely to result in what you are aspiring to. This way, you can anticipate some of possible negative results of your vision and adjust accordingly before they come to pass. Let's say you create a vision of living in California. You are attracted to the warmth, the sun, the ocean, and you can just see yourself rollerblading along the water. Before selling everything and moving, you might want to use simulation as a reality check. Another way of using simulation is to ask yourself, "What will this vision bring me?" That way you can be sure that it's what you really want.

Recognition and simulation, when practiced regularly, result in the apparently effortless "knowing" that we call intuition. But it's like a muscle: Use it or lose it.

IMAGINING THE POSSIBILITIES:
PERSONAL VISIONING EXERCISES

There are numerous ways to create a personal vision, and many articles and book chapters are devoted to the topic. Here, I want to offer three alternatives to get you started. The first involves an exercise that leads to the creation of a vision statement. I've used variations of this with many people, both with individuals and groups. The second is an imagery exercise that you can do alone or with a partner. The third involves the creation of a poster that visually depicts your vision. Choose the one you are drawn to for your first attempt. If you feel especially motivated, you can link all three together, starting with the first and proceeding through them all, preferably in more than one sitting.

EXERCISE ONE: FUTURE VISION

Imagine that you went to sleep last night and woke up this morning several years in the future. Get clear on what date you're imagining and really project yourself into that future. You might even close your eyes. These few years have been really positive for you and your loved ones, the best you can think of. Describe some of the highlights: What happened? Who was involved? Where were you? What did it feel like? Be as specific as possible and allow the images to come, even if they aren't "realistic." You can do your editing and censoring later. Once you've got a clear idea of the elements of your desired future, bring yourself back to the present and write down what came to you. Initially you may have random thoughts and images. Let them come to mind. As a second step, you might want to organize these into categories such as family and friends, significant other, personal growth, fun, physical environment, career, health, and finances.

Sharing your vision with other people is a way to strengthen it. Find someone you know who will be encouraging, not judgmental. Share your vision with them. Invite them to ask you questions as a way to add even greater specificity.

EXERCISE TWO: AN IDEAL DAY

A powerful way to create a personal vision is an imagery exercise in which you envision an ideal day in your life. The basic instruction is as follows: "Describe in detail a day that would be perfect if it represented your usual days—not a vacation or an exception but the way you'd like your life to be all the time. Live that day in the present tense and in detail, identifying where you find yourself, what you do, who you spend time with—from the moment you get up in the morning until the time you go to bed."

If you do this alone, write down all the details as soon as you are finished with the visioning process. Include everything you "saw." No detail is too small to be a clue to your vision. What time did you wake up? Were you woken by an alarm or by the loving kiss of a partner? What did you eat for dinner? Who prepared the meal? And so on.

If you do this exercise with a partner, he or she can help you with the visualization by guiding your through the day one step at a time, gently prompting you to imagine the details through a series of questions.

This exercise can also be done jointly with other people, but it's probably best not done *for* other people. Even people who are very close to another person, such as parents, risk having some version of their own vision substitute for another's. When you are creating a vision for someone who has substantial impairments, it is still possible to guide them through some form of this process, paying close attention to their reactions. I once participated in a conference on person-centered planning for people with disabilities. Part of the event involved creating a plan with and for a number of individuals with disabilities. In the group I was in, the person with whom we created the plan had an image of a kitchen window out of which she could see grass and trees. Living in the country and having a yard became one element of her vision, even though she had not articulated that verbally.

Exercise three: vision poster

Go to an art store or office supply store and purchase a large piece of poster paper, a glue stick, a box of multi-colored markers or crayons, and any other supplies that catch your eye. Some people like the glitter gel pens, and others prefer stickers; choose whatever you feel will liberate your vision. If you have young children, you may already have many of these supplies on hand. Gather together spare catalogues and/or magazines, issues that you don't mind cutting up. Find a pair of scissors. Set aside an hour or so (this will probably be the hardest part), find a spot in your home where you will be relatively undisturbed, and put on some relaxing music. Gather all your supplies together. At the top of your paper, write what it is you want to focus on. It could be "my vision" or "a vision for our family." This helps you to focus. Now start cutting out pictures that appeal to you. If words or phrases come to mind, jot them down on scrap paper. If images appear, draw them on your poster. When you feel you are ready, start writing the phrases on the poster paper and gluing the pictures. Some people suggest that you immediately put this away and let the "visioning magic" work on you subconsciously. I prefer to post my vision somewhere I can see it on a regular basis.

GUIDELINES FOR A COMPELLING VISION

So, you now have a Personal Vision. Let's run it through our litmus test:

- Is it unique? Can you see the specific details that make it yours and not anyone else's?
- Does it make you smile? When you think of the life you've envisioned, do you feel positive energy? If not, you'll abandon it before you even start.
- Is it expansive? Do you realize your vision in such a way that others' lives are improved too?
- Can you imagine concrete things you can do every day to bring your vision into existence?
- Does working toward this vision bring out the best in everyone involved, including you?
- And finally, is it something you can share with others, whether it's through words, pictures, music, or poetry? Because the next step after creating a personal vision is creating shared vision.

VISION AND YOUR ROLE AS A LEADER

As mentioned earlier, one essential task of a leader is to create a context for the formation of a shared vision. That doesn't necessarily mean that your work entails enlisting people to buy in to *your* vision, no matter how tempting that may be. People need to find something inside themselves that resonates with the vision "out there" in order to be more than superficially committed to working toward it. And the more challenging the vision, the more significant the investment needs to be. Shared vision connects people, binds them together by a common aspiration. Shared vision provides the focus and energy for learning, motivating people to learn in order to accomplish something that matters to them.

Shared vision is the catalytic force for change. It's the fuel that moves people from the current to the future state. Peter Senge likens this to the tension generated when one stretches a rubber band: "What does tension seek? Resolution or release. There are only two possible ways for the tension to resolve itself: pull reality toward the vision or pull the vision

30

toward reality. Which occurs will depend on whether we hold steady to the vision." [19]

Here are some suggestions for helping to create conditions that support the formation of a shared vision:

- Develop your own personal vision and a vision for your sphere of influence (your family, your department, your neighborhood, your church). You can use the results of one or more of the exercises above.
- Talk with others about what you have been doing. Encourage them to create their own personal visions and share them with one another. This can be a great activity to do as a family.
- Seek alignment, not agreement. In other words, encourage different perspectives, don't suppress them. Ask people to articulate their differences and why they came to hold those views. For example, if you develop a set of personal vision statements among the members of your family, you are likely to find that there are differences. One member might say, "I envision living in a warm, sunny climate." Another might say, "I want to live in this house until I get old" (and it happens to be in New England). Rather than disagreeing over whose vision is better or whose vision will "win," think about the areas of overlap. Maybe taking a trip to a warm climate every winter would work for everyone.
- Focus on commonalities more than differences. This is similar to the suggestion above. My husband is interested in retiring close to his sixty-fifth birthday, and I have no interest in retiring. But we do agree on many aspects of our desired lifestyle in our older years.
- Expect and nurture reverence for each other.
- Avoid communicating an air of judgment. One of Stephen Covey's *7 Habits* is "Seek first to understand, then to be understood."
- Consider using an *interim vision* to build momentum. Maybe your long-term vision is truly expansive, a bit scary to even imagine getting close to. What can you work toward that would create energy and success that can serve as a platform for even greater accomplishment? This is similar to the "first steps" in the Dannemiller Tyson change formula.
- Invite people to express themselves using a variety of means (poetry, art, music, movement), not just words.

- Appeal to people's values, interests, hopes, and dreams. Vision is not just an idea or abstraction.
- Use language that is alive, resonant, compelling. It helps to describe your vision in the present tense, to use sensory details, as well as to describe what it feels like to be living this vision.

THE CHALLENGES OF CREATING A POSITIVE VISION

In spite of the fact that personal and shared visions have great potency and are an essential aspect of leadership, they do not always emerge easily. As mentioned earlier, if there is nothing in your current reality to suggest what a compelling future might look like, it can be difficult to get a clear image in your mind. When I first started working in the disability field, it was almost inconceivable to envision that people with severe disabilities might live in the community instead of in institutions. Even today, that idea is hard to imagine in some locales. Not so long ago, the concept of "recovery" for people with psychiatric disabilities was unheard of. Both of these developments, and many others that have occurred in the past fifty years, occurred because some people took a leap of faith in spite of the scarcity of examples. Once examples followed, many other such developments could be envisioned and manifested.

In addition to a scarcity of examples, you often find that naysayers are people in positions of authority. I have heard so many stories—and you probably have, as well—of families who were told by their doctor that their child would never live past childhood, so planning for the future would be unnecessary. I've witnessed people with psychiatric disabilities clearly envision being meaningfully engaged in their community—going to the theater, taking cooking classes, holding a job—and had their staff discourage the aspiration as "unrealistic." And because one's vision is often initially quite fragile, it can easily be squashed by strong voices of judgment, especially from those in positions of authority.

When you meet opposition from such people, keep in mind that they have their own perspective and interests. Many of the people who are invested in current reality benefit from that current reality. Why would they want to rock the boat? It might call for extra work or change things for them. It might also offer an implicit critique of what went before and thus of those who supported that reality.

Even without external resistance, it can sometimes be challenging to dream of things that never were. We are not necessarily sure what would make a difference or how to focus our efforts. How can I be confident about where to apply my effort in a way that is likely to bear fruit? What results do I actually want? How will I know those results are worth working toward? These are critical questions, and the answers are not always obvious. One reason is that we live in such a consumer culture that we have often lost touch with our fundamental needs, and perhaps those of the people we care about. For example, families often invest huge amounts of energy advocating for services for their loved ones. When we focus our energy on increased funding or more services, we are behaving as dutiful consumers: I have a headache, so I go buy a product or a service; I have a disability, so I go buy a product or a service. But is that product or service actually going to enable you to realize your vision?

Here's an example: Cheryl is in ninth grade, a freshman in high school. As her mother, you want to ensure that she has the best life possible. In order to accomplish this, should the focus of your leadership be to attain a high quality academic program for her? Is it to assure that she has a group of friends to sit with at lunch? Or is it that she has a detailed Individual Educational Plan (IEP) that clearly documents what goals she is to achieve by the end of the year and what resources will be committed to achieving those goals? Of course, none of these are mutually exclusive. However, in my experience, families often put a great deal of energy into ensuring that the IEP crosses every *t* and dots every *i*. Having a solid IEP is a good thing—as a means to the end you are working to accomplish—but it's just a means. So much effort and energy go into securing the means that we can forget what it's intended to bring about. As some of my colleagues who teach person-centered planning are fond of saying, "A plan is not a life."

THE VISION DILEMMA

So far we have talked about the importance of having a clear, compelling personal vision and the role of the leader in creating shared vision. What happens when those two do not square up? Do you abandon your personal vision in favor of the group's shared vision, or do you steadfastly hold to your personal vision, whether or not others buy in?

This is a practical leadership dilemma because in order to engage in the "activity of mobilizing people to work toward a desired future that not only meets people's needs but elevates them," you need other people. Further, you need the willing enlistment of other people, which suggests that finding common ground is a key leadership activity.

Finding common ground doesn't necessarily mean compromising your own beliefs about what is most important. There are different levels of engagement in creating a shared vision. Depending on the context and who you are trying to engage, you may need to start by piecing together the common elements of everyone's vision into an adequately compelling shared vision. That is what many coalitions and advocacy groups do. For example, when trying to influence legislation, it is often advantageous for groups with a variety of beliefs to band together. None of them give up their deeply held beliefs but they all are committed enough to the passage of the legislation—and see it in their group's best interests—to form a shared vision, at least for the short run. This kind of shared vision is essentially pragmatic and may not hold together over the long-term, but it does have practical advantages.

If you have a particularly strong and focused shared vision and have yet to recruit a constituency, a useful strategy is to recruit people who already hold a similar vision rather than try to influence or shape your constituents. In a sense you are serving as a beacon to attract like-minded people. One way of accomplishing this is to communicate your vision regularly to others, and ask them how it fits with their own. Sometimes your vision will resonate with others, even when they have not yet clearly articulated their own.

Finally, curiosity and openness are two qualities crucial to addressing the vision dilemma. Granted, you have put much of yourself into articulating your own vision. But other people have equally compelling visions that they have worked hard to articulate. Try to be curious about what circumstances inspired the vision of other people, even if—and maybe *especially* if—it is different from or even contradictory to your own.

A PRACTICAL VISIONING EXERCISE TO DO WITH OTHERS

There are many ways to engage people in the creation of a shared vision. What is important is that the process evokes the four attributes of vision described earlier: future orientation, clarity of the image, ideals and standards of excellence, and uniqueness. I often use an exercise that combines elements of several visioning exercises I have participated in or read about. It's called "magazine-article vision exercise":

1. Ask the group to project themselves into the future. The time frame depends on the ambitiousness of their aspirations, but it should be an imaginable time frame, perhaps one to three years. Have them imagine themselves gathered together on the date they identify.
2. Tell them to imagine that the group has worked hard during this period to bring into existence conditions that would contribute

to the vision being realized, and they are gathered to celebrate. Ask them to clearly imagine what they are celebrating, as if it has happened.

3.	To raise the stakes, you can add a twist, "Now further imagine that your group has been chosen as the subject of a national magazine article and that the reporter is coming to interview you about your accomplishments. Please describe the results of all your efforts as though they have already happened."

4.	At this point, people are usually ready to describe the elements of their vision, and they can do so with vividness and clarity. If people are vague in their description, I ask them to describe colors, sounds, smells, and other details. Once the initial flurry of energy diminishes, ask people if there is anything missing. I sometimes like to draw images that depict what people are saying, but it's up to you how you want to capture it. I do recommend having a record that everyone in the group can see rather than writing it down by yourself or not keeping a record at all.

5.	Once this is complete, you might ask people how they are feeling. In my experience, people often reply that they are energized, motivated, and (sometimes) overwhelmed.

This exercise works because it requires people to project themselves into the future and reflect back. This establishes the future orientation and clarity of the image. Uniqueness is accomplished by pushing people for greater specificity and imagining the reporter is interviewing us to learn about our accomplishments. Sometimes, people need to be challenged to stretch toward their ideals and standards of excellence if the vision sounds too much like the status quo.

Another component to this visioning exercise is the link between shared vision and each member's personal vision. This is a good way to ensure that people are invested in the shared vision and are not just going through the motions with the group. The connection between each member's personal vision and the shared vision is the most likely predictor that there will be progress. I have worked with groups that have enthusiastically created a shared vision, goals, objectives, time frames, and even responsible parties—only to reconvene six months later with no accomplishments! Having had that experience a couple of times, I am much more committed to a conscious process of linking each member's personal vision with the shared vision they create. One way that can be done is to create a shared vision and then ask each member to talk about what realization of that will bring to them personally. What are the costs and benefits to them as an individual?

THE BENEFITS OF FALLING SHORT

Karlene Shea is fond of saying: "If you reach for the stars, you'll make it to the top of the mountain. If you reach for the top of the mountain, you'll only make it halfway to the top. If you reach for halfway up the mountain, you'll never get off the ground." A vision, by definition, is an image of the ideal. It's like the North Star, something that orients you but that you don't necessarily achieve. In fact, one perspective is that if you don't fall short, you have not reached high enough.

At the same time, working toward a vision should lead to tangible results and progress. It should be possible to determine whether you are closer to your vision today than you were yesterday. One way to ensure that you are moving toward your vision is to set clear goals. Goals are the measurable and achievable steps you take to work toward realizing your vision. You might have a vision of a world without prejudice and a goal to help elect a black, Hispanic, or woman president of the United States.

One way to link vision with goals is to keep your focus on what is most fundamental and set goals that support that. Returning to the example of Cheryl, the ninth grader: if your vision is for her to be happy and have a life that is rich and rewarding, you'll need to figure out what would enable that to happen. Friends? A job? A good education? It might be different for different people. Once you're clear about what is most fundamental, then you create goals around those things. This is easier said than done, because it's often hard to know what will actually bring us what we want.

However, it's a worthwhile exercise because measuring progress is a powerful motivator. Knowing that you have successfully accomplished something you set out to do spurs you on to set more goals. Knowing that you have fallen short can be the catalyst for renewed effort or possibly for a revision of the goal or the approach to reaching that goal. Leadership is as much about failing as it is about succeeding. In fact, many of the most notable leaders have had lives characterized by a series of failures punctuated by a handful of spectacular successes. The key is to learn from both failures and successes.

When taking stock of whether you are making progress, it's helpful to gather the perspectives of a variety of involved people, not to just do it on your own. Because progress is a multifaceted thing, you may find that others can spot accomplishments where you feel frustration. It may also be that others can see when the goal needs to be revised in order to more accurately reflect your vision. And make sure to hold periodic celebrations as well as evaluations. Although evaluation and judgment are quite commonplace, taking the time to celebrate happens so rarely.

WHAT IF YOU LOSE FAITH?

It is entirely likely that somewhere on the journey toward realizing your vision, you will waver in confidence, succumb to exhaustion, or lose faith that the vision can be realized—or is even *worth* realizing. This is natural. In another chapter, the topics of renewal and revitalization are addressed more extensively, but here are some suggestions that relate specifically to the loss of faith in your vision.

- *Rededicate yourself to the source of your original vision.* All of us have a set of core values and commitments that motivate us and inspire our vision. In the course of living out these values and commitments, many successful leaders find themselves taking on broader responsibilities, only to wake up one day and discover that they are no longer as connected to what initially inspired them to become leaders. Families who become so active in working toward goals that would positively impact on hundreds of lives may find that they no longer take the time as frequently to hang out with their son with disabilities. Advocates who were inspired to take leadership because they encountered injustices in the lives of specific individuals find they can easily lose touch with those individuals in the effort to have a broader impact. You might start asking yourself, "And why, exactly, am I doing this?" If so, what you need may be to get back in touch with those people who inspired you to take on a leadership role in the first place.
- *Take a break.* Maybe you have been too immersed in the issues; you've lost perspective, can't see the big picture. A break can be very renewing, whether you go on a vacation or just take a walk. Don't worry, the work will still be there waiting for you.
- *Recruit others to take the lead, temporarily or forever.* It's important to know when it's time to retire. Even if you still passionately want to bring about your vision, it may be time to turn things over to other people. Perhaps you can play the role of a mentor or coach but not in an active leadership role. That's a huge contribution, and it enables you to continue

working toward your vision without becoming cynical or discouraged.

- *Review and refresh your vision.* Over time, things change—in the world and inside ourselves. What was an inspiring vision twenty years ago may feel a bit stale over time. Is it time to set a new benchmark, climb a higher mountain, or look at the whole situation in a new way? We can often operate on autopilot about our beliefs and aspirations if we don't periodically update and refresh them. For example, for many years I worked to promote social integration for people with disabilities as if it was an end in itself. A few years ago, I realized that social integration is, instead, a means to a deeper end, that of enabling people with disabilities to use their gifts and develop their potential so they can be contributing members of community life. That goes way beyond social integration and calls for a whole new way of thinking about goals and strategies that elevates the aspiration to a higher level.

In this chapter, we've explored the critical role of vision to the leadership journey—both personal vision and shared vision. We've looked at some of the challenges of creating a clear vision and have offered some strategies that might help. In the next chapter, we will continue to delve more deeply into the topic of leadership by examining what leaders really do. One concluding question that might serve to link vision to the day-to-day realities of leadership is this: How do you have to live each day in order to move toward your vision?

CHAPTER 4
WHAT DO LEADERS ACTUALLY DO?

INTRODUCTION

Up to this point, we have explored what leadership is, why one might want to lead (or not!), and the power of vision to create momentum toward the realization of one's aspirations. But the nitty-gritty, day-to-day *work* of leadership has not yet been addressed. Simply stated, the work of leadership involves mobilizing people to work toward a desired future. There are concrete things leaders do with their people in order to bring this about. That is the focus of this chapter.

WHERE DO I START?

Years ago, I attended a retreat called "The Courage to Teach." The retreat was facilitated by Parker Palmer, a mentor of mine, and it focused on the relationship between the "inner teacher" and one's outer, active life. We read a poem by Marge Piercy and discussed its implications for how we make a difference in the world. Parker began the discussion by inviting us to reflect on how Rosa Parks and Vaclav Havel acted as leaders. He then shared his image that "they planted the seed of true self into the soil of possibility. The way things change is the way nature grows, not so much what we *make* happen, but the organic growth into full possibility."

Piercy's poem reminds us that this work happens over time, often underground, and that it is often not neat and straightforward—with a beginning, middle, and end. I invite you to read her poem and reflect on the questions that follow.

"The Seven of Pentacles"

Under a sky the color of pea soup
she is looking at her work growing away there
actively, thickly like grapevines or pole beans
as things grow in the real world, slowly enough.
If you tend them properly, if you mulch, if you water,
if you provide birds that eat insects a home and winter food,
if the sun shines and you pick off caterpillars,
if the praying mantis comes and the ladybugs and the bees,
then the plants flourish, but at their own internal clock.

Connections are made slowly, sometimes they grow
underground.
You cannot tell always by looking what is happening.
More than half a tree is spread out in the soil under your feet.
Penetrate quietly as the earthworm that blows no trumpet.
Fight persistently as the creeper that brings down the tree.
Spread like the squash plant that overruns the garden.
Gnaw in the dark and use the sun to make sugar.

Weave real connections, create real nodes, build real houses.
Live a life you can endure: make love that is loving.
Keep tangling and interweaving and taking more in,
a thicket and bramble wilderness to the outside but to us
interconnected with rabbit runs and burrows and lairs.

Live as if you liked yourself, and it may happen:
reach out, keep reaching out, keep bringing in.
This is how we are going to live for a long time: not always,
for every gardener knows that after the digging, after
the planting,
after the long season of tending and growth, the harvest comes.[20]

1. Do any of the images in the poem shed light on the question,
   "What do leaders do"?
2. How might you view your leadership if you saw what you are
   doing as stewarding "organic growth into full possibility"?
3. Is there something you are tending that is flourishing but "at
   its own internal clock"? How do you respond? How does it
   make you feel?

4. What is the harvest in the leadership work you are engaged in?

The image of leadership as tending to nature is a reminder that we serve as stewards, not as the all-powerful creators of the future we aspire to. It would be like boasting that I *created* the stunning spray of white flowers on the orchid plant in my living room merely because I watered and fed it regularly. As stewards, we assume responsibility and accountability, but we don't actually control much of the outcome of the work of leadership. People sometimes refer to their efforts to get a group of people to go in the same direction as "like herding cats." To me, that's a pretty good job description of leadership. You can influence, but rarely do you control.

If we serve as stewards, what is it that we are actually stewards of? The first thing that comes to mind is *relationships.* Forming, strengthening, mending relationships is a huge part of the work of leadership. Not only relationships between people, although that is critical. But also relationship between people and ideas, one idea and another, and the relationship between cause and effect. Much of leadership has to do with the cultivation of relationships.

The next thing we are stewards of is *time.* When we are in leadership roles, we have a great deal of responsibility to work with time in an effective way. Not only does the way we use time have an impact on our effectiveness, but it also impacts how well other people are able to work.

Related to time are *priorities.* In leadership roles, we have a huge influence on how people define what is most important and, consequently, what they spend time doing. But being a steward of priorities involves more than merely telling people what to focus on. It also involves being attuned to where people's attention tends to focus and finding a way to link priorities to the issues people are inclined to focus on.

We are also stewards of *emotions* that can facilitate our capacity to accomplish the work of leadership or to impede it. Being attuned to the emotions of the individuals and groups you work with can be very important, not necessarily in a solicitous way—sometimes it is perfectly appropriate for there to be anger, sadness, or grief—but as a way of gauging whether the emotions of the group are in sync with the work that needs to occur.

And then we are stewards of *resources,* meaning money and materials. Although it is possible to exercise leadership with minimal resources, most often it helps to have access to some resources in order to work toward your vision. If you are planning to build a home, for example, it would be rather risky to get really clear on your vision without putting together a materials list and a budget. You'd risk getting halfway through the building process and running out of money or materials.

Each leader exercises this stewardship in a personal way. How you go about doing the work of leadership is very much related to who you are. In spite of all the books on how to be a leader, ultimately it comes down to the relationship between who you are, who your constituents are, and what needs doing. There is no "one right way" to exercise leadership. However, there are some things leaders *do* to mobilize people to work toward a desired future that are relatively consistent. These will be explored in more detail below.

Before describing the work of leadership in more detail, I'd like you to bring to mind a leadership experience you participated in. This can provide some concrete examples as we continue to explore what leaders actually do.

Keeping in mind the definition of leadership presented earlier in this book, think back over the past two weeks. If it helps, you might pull out your calendar and take a look at what you did over this period of time. Pick one event or activity where you participated in exercising leadership, whether it was individually or as part of a group. It doesn't have to be anything big or complicated. Jot down some notes describing the experience. As we go along, you will periodically be invited to reflect on your experience in relation to what we are focusing on.

THE WORK OF LEADERSHIP

Up to this point, the stage has been set for thinking of leadership as an organic—not mechanical—process and for thinking of leaders as stewards of the "materials" needed to do the work. But we have not yet identified what it is that leaders actually do. I propose that there are four main activities of leadership. These are:

- Identifying the adaptive challenge
- Engaging people to create a shared vision that each buys into
- Ensuring that people are organized to work productively
- Giving work back to the people

Although there is no rigid sequence for engaging in these activities—some may even happen simultaneously—the work of leadership generally starts by asking "What are we going to work on?" He then proceeds to gain the buy-in of stakeholders followed by forging a set of relationships and a framework that enables people to work toward their vision.

IDENTIFYING THE ADAPTIVE CHALLENGE

You may remember the Dannemiller-Tyson change formula presented in the previous chapter: conditions are conducive to change when the sum of Dissatisfaction, Vision, and First steps is greater than Resistance ($D + V + F > R$). One of the first things a leader needs to do is to use dissatisfaction with the current situation to help people frame a challenge that gets them started on addressing what is truly important. In order to do this, it can be useful to distinguish among three *different kinds of leadership challenges:*[21]

1. *Where existing authority/expertise can both define and remedy the problem.* An example of this might be a bridge that is structurally unsound. Engineers conduct a series of tests to determine that it is unsound, and they make plans to rebuild or shore up the bridge.

2. *Where the problem is definable but no clear solution is available.* People must learn together to create a solution. Continuing with the bridge example: on Martha's Vineyard at the time of this writing, there is a drawbridge that is old and unsound located on a busy road between two towns. The bridge spans the opening between Lagoon Pond (where a number of residents dock their boats) and the Vineyard Haven Harbor. There is much discussion about the best way to rebuild the bridge in order to maximize functional, aesthetic, and environmental considerations. Not surprisingly, there are many points of view on this issue, and although there is little disagreement with the fact that the bridge is unsound and something must be done, there are many perspectives on what the course of action should be.

3. *Where learning is required both to define the problem and to discover and implement solutions.* For example, how do we learn how to "bridge" two or more cultures? What is at the core of our mistrust and suspicion of people we define as different? And what solutions might emerge?

It can be tempting to treat all three of these leadership challenges as if they require the same kind of response: to find the right experts who will tell us what to do so we can do it. But it's more complicated than that. Some leadership challenges require changes in values, behavior, or a reconciliation between differing values or behavior. Still others call for

43

new learning. That's work that *we* have to do, rather than merely turning to an expert to be given the answer. Even if an expert did give us the answers, we might not take action because we have conflicting values or entrenched patterns of behavior. Your doctor can tell you to lose weight or stop smoking, but those things don't happen just because she gives you good advice. You have to reconcile your competing values and change your entrenched patterns of behavior.

Actually, when we treat complex leadership challenges with simple or short-term solutions, we can make the problem worse. One example of this is excessive use of out-of-district educational placements for youth with disabilities. This "out of sight, out of mind" response deals with a symptom of the problem, but some of the unintended consequences include an increase in special education costs, increased resentment of the money spent on special ed, failure to increase the schools' capacity to successfully integrate youth with disabilities, and a widening of the chasm between youth with and without special needs—all while creating the perception that the problem is being "solved."

The terms *adaptive challenge* and *adaptive work* were coined by Ron Heifetz, who writes, "Adaptive work consists of the learning required to address conflicts in the values people hold, or to diminish the gap between the values people stand for and the reality they face. Adaptive work requires a change in values, beliefs, or behavior."[22] He notes that an important part of the work of leadership is to first uncover the underlying tensions and contradictions that produce an adaptive challenge. Then the work requires identifying what matters most, in what balance, and with which trade-offs. This is not easy. Often there is controversy and conflict surrounding these kinds of challenges. Sometimes there is longstanding animosity between the stakeholders. The real issue may not even have been identified, or there may be numerous real issues. Even when the issue has been sufficiently identified, there may be no apparent answers. At the same time, there is the temptation to pick a course of action—any course of action—and proceed, rather than live with uncertainty and ambiguity.

A key principle for those in leadership roles who are concerned with helping effectively frame these challenges is that doing so requires taking a bird's-eye view. Rather than being invested in a particular perspective, the question is, "What's the greater good?" A useful exercise is to practice taking the perspectives of others who hold different points of view. For example, imagine you are trying to encourage a mother who is reluctant to let her teenager with a disability have his own paper route. First, suspend your own point of view. Now, try to see the situation from the mother's perspective. Then try to see it from the teen's perspective. Go through each of the key people who have a role in this issue in turn, and then see if you can come up with an answer to the question, "What's the greater good in this situation?" In this example, the adaptive challenge may be finding a way to support the increasing independence of the teen while honoring the parents' legitimate concern for his safety.

Identifying and addressing adaptive challenges is more than just an intellectual exercise. There is a reason why the status quo exists! The underlying contradictions might be so large that it's easier to keep things as they are. Perhaps the magnitude of the change needed is overwhelming, or the potential implications of the change for individual stakeholders are difficult to embrace. It can be helpful to explore these questions: "What is the worst that can happen if we do commit to change? What are the consequences of *not* changing?"

Before we move on to the next key activity of leadership, take a minute to reflect on how you would describe the adaptive challenge associated with the leadership experience you remembered earlier in this chapter. What was at stake? What were people really working to address? What would you describe as the greater good?

In the next section, we will explore another key activity of leadership: engaging people to create a shared vision that each member buys into.

Engaging People to Create a Shared Vision That Each Member Buys Into

This aspect of the work of leadership has been addressed at length in the preceding chapter. It's critically important that there is shared vision, and that people are fully invested in working toward that vision. Most adaptive challenges will require significant commitment and even sacrifice to produce real results. That is part of the reason why we often apply simple solutions to complex problems: It's easier to create a committee to study the problem, allocate some resources, or develop a plan than it is to wrestle with the changes in values and behaviors necessary to address most fundamental challenges. Thus, in order to create and sustain momentum on significant issues, strong motivation needs to be generated from those who will be called upon to do the work.

Although this can be done by threats of punishment and reprisal, it is both more useful and more ethical to create momentum by tapping into members' personal values and interests. So often in the human service field, self-interest is perceived as a negative thing. And yet some of the most dedicated leaders acknowledge that their commitment is fueled by personal interest. Remember Virginia, who, in chapter 2, was quoted as saying, "It's all about my daughter"? The key thing here is to work with people to determine what's in it for them. And it doesn't need to be fame or glory or making sure a loved one gets services. Often it's the sense that one is contributing to making the world a better place or giving back when one has received help.

The creation of this shared vision—or even the enlistment of others to buy into *your* vision—often has deeper work associated with it: that of helping those you are leading to articulate their own personal values. When you hold forth the possibility that an overworked, underpaid teacher might contribute to working toward the vision of full inclusion for your child, your work is to tap into that teacher's deeper source of positive motivation for doing the work he does. In order to do this, you will need to relate to that teacher with compassion rather than as an enemy who is blocking your child from having a good life. If you've had difficult experiences with this teacher, or with teachers in general, compassion is a hard place to come from. But it's highly unlikely that, as a leader, you will be able to accomplish this aspect of the work of leadership without considerable compassion.

ENSURING THAT PEOPLE ARE ORGANIZED
TO WORK PRODUCTIVELY

Once the adaptive challenge has been identified and a shared vision created, the work of leadership focuses on creating arrangements that enable people to work productively. It's not enough to know what the issue is and what you want the world to look like. These are critical aspects of leadership. However, in order to accomplish results, you have to work with people's time, talents, energy, and personalities. Have you ever joined a group— enthusiastic about its mission and purpose, willing to contribute your time and talent to further the purpose of that group—only to find that there does not seem to be a place for you? Or perhaps you've been involved in an organization that is so hell-bent on accomplishing its purpose that it burns out the contributing members in short order. Equally frustrating are groups with a compelling purpose but an unworkable structure to accomplish that purpose.

All of these situations illustrate how critical it is to have arrangements that ensure people are working productively. Time after time, the accomplishment of a group's laudable purpose is hampered by inadequate leadership when it comes to deploying people.

There are at least four practices that help people work productively:

- Ensuring that people's skills and talents are "plugged in"
- Ensuring that there is a sense of trust and teamwork
- Ensuring that people have an appropriate sense of urgency
- Ensuring that the work is paced effectively

Before I describe each of these in more detail, think of a group that you joined or became involved with that had a purpose you were committed to. Spend a few minutes exploring the following questions:

1. When you first got involved with the group, was it readily apparent how you might make a contribution? If so, how did that make you feel, and what was the result? If not, how did that make you feel, and what was the result? What did you do?
2. When you have been part of a group where there is a lack of trust and sense of teamwork, what are the consequences? How does trust actually get created?
3. Was there a time when you were part of a group that had not paced its work in a reasonable way? What were the effects? Have you ever been involved with a group that lacked the sense of urgency that seemed appropriate to its purpose? What were the effects?

ENSURING THAT PEOPLE'S SKILLS AND TALENTS ARE "PLUGGED IN"

A critical aspect of sustaining engagement in a group is the availability of various roles that can be filled by members and a clear process for connecting appropriate people to those roles. In particular, new members of a group are often uncertain about how the group operates and are tentative about where they fit in. Developing and maintaining ways of shepherding new people into relevant roles is a critical function of leadership. If people are left to their own devices for too long, the strong and assertive people will find a place, and others will drift away. Even long-term participants benefit from support to ensure that they are making a genuine contribution to the work of the group.

Sometimes this means creating opportunities that are not obvious or appear to be inefficient or redundant. A political campaign is a good example. There are roles for fundraisers, hosts, office workers, and marketing and public-relations people. There are even roles for people who like to smile and wave, holding a sign. For people who want to play a part but can't commit a great deal of time, there are placards to place on lawns, checks to write, petitions to sign, and so on. Whoever came up with the structure of a political campaign was brilliant at thinking, *How many different kinds of jobs can we create to keep people engaged?* And of course, such a campaign culminates with the final important role: voting!

Not only is it important to have available a variety of roles in which to steer people, but it is also key that the roles suit the talents and skills of those who fill them. This is a delicate and tricky process, because sometimes people volunteer to fill roles for which they are ill-suited. In that case, it needs to be discerned whether some kind of education or coaching might narrow the gap between a person's capacity and what's called for or whether a better strategy would be to gently steer the person into a role that is more suitable. This depends on how important the role is, how public the results will be, and other considerations of that sort.

Ensuring that there is a sense of trust and teamwork

This is one aspect of the work of leadership that is both glaringly obvious and challenging to carry out in real life. Most of us must work with others to produce the results we want. But just because we must work together doesn't mean we are a "team" in the fullest sense of the word. Building and sustaining a team whose members trust one another, work collaboratively, and accomplish the desired results is the subject of many books, training sessions, and consulting engagements—and still people often find themselves challenged in their work together.

In my experience, fundamental to working well as a team is a strong sense of trust among team members. This enables other aspects of teamwork to emerge.

What are some things that affect a team's ability to trust one another? Here are some examples.

- Fairness: People on a team want to feel that they are being treated equitably. As individual team members, we live with the tension between self-interest and the collective interest. When team members suspect inequities, self-interest often becomes a dominant consideration ("I'm determined to get my fair share!") which erodes a sense of trust.
- Transparency: This involves being open to scrutiny or critique. It is a building block of trust because people feel like they know what's going on. Secrecy breeds suspicion and mistrust, even if there is nothing unscrupulous going on.

- Honoring different perspectives: Differences are not only inevitable, they are also a potent force for creativity and innovation. Capitalizing on differences while avoiding destructive conflict is important for team functioning and successful accomplishment of goals.

These are a few examples of practices that impact on trust within a team. Skillful leaders pay attention to all of them, although it is not possible to control or manage each of the factors completely. And the work is never-ending, because adjustments must be made when the composition of the group changes or the group takes on a new challenge. Sometimes a group operates very well as a team in the day-to-day handling of routine matters. However, when faced with a crisis or a dramatic challenge, it may find itself needing to regroup.

Ensuring that people have an appropriate sense of urgency

An important aspect of the work of leadership is to continually stay focused on the "desired future" and make adjustments in the timing and pacing of the work done to arrive at that desired future. Instilling an appropriate sense of urgency is one aspect of this.

A simple way of thinking about this is to think of a continuum with a "strong sense of urgency" on one end and a "sense of complacency" on the other end. The leadership challenge is to evaluate what is the most *appropriate* sense of urgency for the circumstances and then to take steps to engage others in that sense.

This is more difficult than it may seem. First, it requires that those in leadership roles be realistic and clear-thinking about the true nature of the situation. This, in turn, calls for the capacity to continue leading even when things are really bad, rather than to shut down and withdraw. It has been said that courage is not the absence of fear; it's the capacity to continue acting in the face of fear. While we may think of courage as a quality most needed in life-or-death situations, it also takes courage to face the difficult circumstances that many organizations get into and continue leading through those.

For example, imagine you joined the board of an organization and were attending your first board meeting. The meeting agenda had to do with planning the future of the organization from a mission and purpose perspective. First, however, routine business needed to be covered, such as a report from the finance committee. The finance committee report states that, nine months into the year, last year's audit was not completed. Accurate information was difficult to gather due to the high turnover of financial people and the reliance on temporary bookkeepers. There was a longstanding deficit that was carried from year to year. Budget forecasts for the existing year fluctuated widely, but a reasonable forecast was a $200,000 loss. Alarmed, you ask the executive director if this is a crisis. He replies in a calm tone, "It's been this way for several years. We think we are making progress on reducing the deficit." As a board member, how confident would you feel, based on the executive director's behavior, that there was an appropriate sense of urgency regarding the organization's financial well-being?

On the other end of the continuum, indiscriminately applying a "strong sense of urgency" becomes the classic Chicken Little syndrome, where *everything* is perceived as a crisis or an impending disaster. This way of leading cannot be sustained for long, because people quickly lose confidence in the leader's judgment. An important characteristic of leadership is the capacity to discriminate among issues in order to apply energy and focus to those that are most fundamental. If those in leadership roles communicate a sense of urgency about every issue, "urgency fatigue" sets in and people stop responding.

In summary, instilling an appropriate sense of urgency has to do with modulating the energy and emotion people bring to the work they are engaged in. Relatedly, leaders also must pay attention to ensuring that the work is paced well, a task that has its own challenges.

ENSURING THAT THE WORK IS PACED EFFECTIVELY

Imagine that you are about to begin running a five-kilometer road race. You know the course, having run it several times while training for the race. You know your physical condition. You have a sense of the weather conditions and other factors (humidity, air quality, the number and fitness of other competitors) that are likely to have an impact on your race. You have a plan in mind about how you are going to run this race—when to hold yourself back, when to go flat out. Once the race starts, that plan is adjusted frequently to respond to conditions you encounter.

Just as pacing is critically important to the successful completion of a road race (or however you define success), it is equally important to the work of leadership. In the leadership arena, pacing the work involves several capacities:

1. Being able to discern when an issue is *ripe* for addressing, that is, when conditions within the environment are conducive to making progress. Such conditions might include the passage of legislation supporting the issue you are working on. Recent media attention is another facilitating condition. Or conditions relevant to your issue might have reached the "tipping point," to use Malcolm Gladwell's expression, which is described as "that magic moment when an idea, trend, or social behavior crosses a threshold, tips, and spreads like wildfire."[23]

2. Being willing to *go slow to go fast*. Often, taking the necessary time to plan, discuss, celebrate, or grieve is critical to the pacing of future work. Skillful leaders develop a sixth sense for when it's time to slow down and focus on the process, not just the outcome.

3. Being able to make adjustments and course corrections in the moment while staying focused on the desired future, just as the runner does in a five-kilometer race. Skillful leadership in this area requires constant adjustment based on respectful feedback and interaction between leaders and followers.

There are consequences when the pacing is not right. Pacing that is too slow leads to boredom, complacency, and the squandering of potential. Pacing that is too rapid can result in diminished performance and a compromise of the more subtle work needed to be effective.

GIVING WORK BACK TO THE PEOPLE

The final aspect of the work of leadership, giving work back to the people, helps to assure that the things you care deeply about will have a life beyond your personal involvement in a leadership role. In a sense, this practice is your legacy for the future.

In addition, giving work back to the people creates opportunities for others to develop their capabilities as leaders, and it serves to build and sustain a commitment on the part of those engaged in the work.

However, just like every aspect of the work of leadership, the practice of giving work back to the people is more challenging than it may seem.

Here's a little quiz.

- *As parents*, you are important advocates for your child. But how much energy have you devoted to ensuring that your child is his or her own best advocate? Or that the teacher or service worker with whom you have a good relationship is doing her part to advance your vision for your child?

- *As group leaders,* it can often be hard to get others to attend meetings, never mind making the phone calls and sending out newsletters. Do you sometimes find yourself doing the work yourself one more time when no one steps up to the plate?
- *As self advocates,* have you sometimes been skeptical of the motivation of a nondisabled person to get involved in your advocacy efforts and decided to stick with other self advocates?
- *As advocates of community membership,* do you have doubts about the willingness of other citizens to commit themselves to working on behalf of people with disabilities? Do you secretly believe that you and your allies are more dedicated to the goals of community membership and inclusion than any other citizens could or would be? How does that secret belief affect your capacity to reach out and engage others?

Every one of these examples would benefit from a conscious and disciplined strategy to give work back to the people. And yet, from the point of view of the main characters, it is completely understandable why it wouldn't be worth making such an effort. Giving work back to the people starts with the confidence that the issues that matter to you could also be of interest to others who would willingly commit to working on them. If you've ever experienced devaluation or marginalization, that can be a big leap of faith. Second, it entails extra work and being willing to let go of the idea that there is one best way to get something done. Third, people can be really resistant and have all sorts of justifications for why they cannot or will not take on more responsibility.

There are proven strategies for giving work back to the people that involve putting the other aspects of the work of leadership into practice. These include:

- Making sure people's skills are plugged in by inviting them to take on responsibility and by appealing to their sense of competence and capability.
- Revisiting your efforts to engage people in a shared vision by reflecting on how invested people are. Perhaps they are not as invested as they need to be in order to follow through with the work of bringing the vision into reality.

- Heightening a sense of urgency in order for people to take on responsibility.

Success at "giving work back to the people" is the litmus test of your success in the other aspects of the work of leadership. And if this isn't a strong aspect of your work as a leader, it will become a self-fulfilling prophecy that "you're the only one who cares."

This has been a challenging chapter to write. Undoubtedly it has also been challenging to read. While it's packed with the nuts and bolts of how to lead, it is still pretty theoretical. One suggestion is to pick one aspect of the work of leadership and really focus on it: how you are applying it, what you are learning, what you agree with, or what you disagree with. By doing that—and keeping notes on what you're finding—you can add your own lessons and examples. Then move on to another aspect of leadership and do the same. What's in this chapter took me many years to learn through integrating personal experience, observing the leadership of others, and much reading. It takes time!

In the next chapter, we will look at some of the common questions and concerns that arise as people exercise leadership.

CHAPTER 5
ADDRESSING LEADERSHIP CHALLENGES

INTRODUCTION

In the previous chapter, we examined the question, "What do leaders do?" We identified and explained the key activities of leadership. For virtually every one of those activities, we pointed out that skillfulness involves good judgment, flexibility, and adaptability to changing circumstances. This chapter will address some of the common questions and concerns raised by people as they go about exercising leadership. Although there are probably many more questions—particularly those that have to do with tactics—these are common questions raised by people I have taught and coached.

"I HAVE REAL DOUBTS ABOUT WHETHER I'M CUT OUT TO BE A LEADER."

As discussed in chapter 1, we often have unconscious models of leadership that we compare ourselves to, usually unfavorably. Early on in our leadership careers, we sometimes feel like impostors, but even seasoned leaders can preoccupy themselves with those traits or characteristics they lack and lose focus on the impact they are seeking to make in the world. Shifting one's attention to the work of leadership is one major strategy for dealing with doubts and misgivings: What work needs doing? Chances are, the work you have taken on is not being done by anyone else, so it's not as important to be perfect as it is to do something useful.

In addition, if you commit yourself to learning from what went well and what didn't go well, you will almost inevitably develop more skill and confidence as you go along. It's all learning! In the meantime, it's helpful to find people who believe in you, who support you, and who can give you good advice.

Finally, if you practice the disciplines of leadership laid out in this book, you will become more skillful in your practice of leadership, and presumably the doubts and uncertainties will fade away.

By the way, having doubts about your leadership is probably a better stance to take than the next one: arrogance.

"I OFTEN FEEL THAT I KNOW BETTER THAN OTHERS WHAT NEEDS TO HAPPEN AND HOW TO DO IT. IT'S HARD FOR ME TO LISTEN TO OTHERS' IDEAS."

Okay, maybe you're not asking this question quite so directly. Maybe your belief that you know best is reflected more in your behavior. This belief suggests that you may have lost sight of the fact that leadership is the relationship between the leader and his/her followers. If you think you know best, that you don't need other people, you might be a prophet or a saint, but it's unlikely you will be able to exercise leadership for long.

It's human to get impatient and to think of one's own point of view as the "right" one. But to mobilize people to work toward a desired future, there need to be give-and-take and regular course corrections based on input from others.

Try not to isolate yourself from your constituents. Stay open to new views, new learning. Discipline yourself to see things from other people's points of view. Take yourself out of your comfort zone and become a beginner again. Become a student of someone you view as less advanced than you; everyone can teach us something. And don't ever forget that followers are as important as leaders.

"ALTHOUGH I WANT TO EXERCISE LEADERSHIP, I GET FEEDBACK FROM OTHERS THAT I HAVE PERSONAL SHORTCOMINGS THAT GET IN THE WAY."

Probably the first thing to do is to figure out what kind of personal shortcomings people are noticing. Some shortcomings reflect a lack of skill or experience. For example, maybe you are not a polished communicator or writer. In these instances, you can try to develop your skills, or you can team up with people who already have those skills. Maybe you do both for a while until you improve.

Other shortcomings fall more in the realm of personality traits. Examples include being disorganized, chronically late, unable to follow through on commitments, or impatient with others. These characteristics may have the tendency to unfavorably affect others you are attempting to work with, leading them to avoid working with you. But if you are serious about the issues you want to address, these traits can be kept in check or compensated for.

Another group of shortcomings are more fundamental and speak to whether you will be successful as a leader. If you are perceived as lacking credibility, integrity, or trustworthiness, it will be difficult to attract and retain constituents. If the feedback you receive falls into this category, it might be useful to do some careful analysis of your actions and the motivations behind them. Do you make promises that you fully intend to fulfill—at the time you make them? Do you operate on the principle that "the end justifies the means"? Do you find it hard to refuse anyone, even if it means making competing commitments? An objective analysis of the impact of your actions can help you to decide if your actions need to change or if you need to let others take on leadership roles. And although the feedback can sometimes be challenging, it's important to stay open to it.

"I AM JUST SO EXHAUSTED AND TIRED OF BATTLING WITH THE WORLD."

Maybe it's time to take a step back and regain your perspective. It might even be time for a break, if you can afford to do so and not lose the gains you have made. Everybody needs to have sources of renewal and ways to regain their energy. If you are dragging through every day, you are depleting more energy than you are renewing. Try to identify some things that give you pleasure, motivation, and enthusiasm. Build those into your life, especially during the most difficult and stressful times. Evaluate the strategies you are using for their effectiveness. It might be time to change your approach.

Maybe you are trying to do too much by yourself. Having allies and collaborators can be a tremendous help. Even if you are all exhausted together, there is something about being in the company of people who share a vision and a cause that offers strength.

You might want to ask yourself if your mind-set is contributing to your exhaustion. People who view life as a series of battles can get so caught up in slogging through the mud that they miss the occasional limousine waiting to take them to their next stop. Although much of the work you have to do is hard, sometimes it's not as hard as we make it out to be.

And maybe it's time to turn the work over to other people, either temporarily or permanently.

"IT SEEMS LIKE I'VE HAD SETBACK AFTER SETBACK. I'M FEELING SO FRUSTRATED."

The first step here would also be to take a step back and regain your perspective. Getting the help of a trusted advisor would be very useful, since you are probably too close and emotionally involved to do the kind of analysis that is necessary at this point. You probably want to look carefully at every aspect of what you are working to accomplish: Are your goals too ambitious? Have you failed to gain buy-in from people who are key to the success of your initiative? Are you trying to move things along too quickly? Are there factors in the external environment that are constraining you, which you haven't sufficiently taken account of? Do you need to improve your skills in certain areas or recruit others who already have the skills?

There are many other questions to consider, but the key is to take a broad view and try to take your feelings out of the analysis, at least for the moment. In order to do that, it can help to do some venting at the beginning and then settle down and look carefully at the situation. The chapter on systems thinking may help you with this.

"NOBODY TAKES ME SERIOUSLY AS A LEADER."

Perhaps the most important question to ask yourself is, "Do *you* take yourself seriously as a leader?" If you care deeply about something and you communicate that to other people, eventually you will attract supporters—especially if you stay focused on the work at hand and develop a track record of serious results. There are many examples of young leaders, people who did not start out with the external trappings of a leader but who made a commitment to produce results in the world and followed through with actions. For example, a young man named Emanuel Tsourounis II, while he was still in elementary school, gathered a group of students to complain to the principal that teachers unfairly gave out punishment during quiet time. The group was so persuasive that the principal made changes in the practice.

Throughout his high school years, Tsourounis worked to increase student representation in his local board of education as well as on the state board of education, among other activities. In his junior year in college, Tsourounis coauthored a book aimed at encouraging youth activism. When he was interviewed for an article in the paper, he said, "No one's going to say to you, 'Come and change something.' If you see something, you have to say, 'This is how it can be improved.' Before you get to that point, you've got to recognize that you are just as capable and important as an adult, as someone in city hall, as a taxpayer."

That message is not relevant only to young people. As families and people with disabilities, you also have been conditioned to believe that you are one-down from the special education administrator, the agency director, and the service coordinator. Being taken seriously starts with yourself.

"I'M TRYING TO HAVE AN IMPACT ON SOMETHING THAT'S IMPORTANT TO ME, BUT I CAN'T GET ENOUGH PEOPLE ON BOARD."

Sometimes you need to start small and take an action that is within your control before other people will join with you. This can serve both as evidence of your commitment to the issue at hand and also as a concrete example for others that something can really be done. Let's say you're interested in helping a friend of yours who has a disability find a job in a museum. You have approached the various employment services providers in your area with the prospect, and none of them seem either willing or able to make that happen. You have several options at that point. You can continue trying to persuade the agencies that this is the right thing to do. You can give up and let your friend fill one of the jobs an agency *is* able to find for him. Or you can help him yourself. None of these are necessarily right or wrong. However, the third option does enable you to have the kind of impact you are seeking more directly. If you are successful, you might eventually approach an open-minded agency with the proposal that they take responsibility for ongoing support, if necessary.

This approach—taking personal responsibility to bring something you care about into existence—is how virtually all developments in service get started. For example, in the 1930s, families of individuals with developmental disabilities started to network in an effort to develop services for their children. The first national meeting of parents was convened in September 1950 in Minneapolis, Minnesota, and evolved into an organization called the Association for Retarded Children (ARC). Thanks in part to high-profile support from individuals—such as President John F. Kennedy, who had a sister with developmental disabilities—community services were developed, and citizens began reevaluating their views about people with developmental disabilities and their families.

The L'Arche Movement, founded by Jean Vanier in 1964, is another example. L'Arche began when Jean Vanier invited two men living in an institution in France to leave the institution and share their lives with him in his home. Today, L'Arche Communities bring together people, some with developmental disabilities and some without, who choose to share their lives by living together in faith-based communities. There are communities in several countries around the world.

In each of these examples, people took action without waiting to convince others to join them. Along the way, many others became engaged or the developments would not have occurred. It's not that you don't need other people; it's that you often don't need others to set things in motion.

"WE JUST HAD A BIG SETBACK."

We already looked at this challenge from the personal point of view earlier. I recommended taking a step back and regaining your perspective. That's the work you need to do as a leader in order to be responsive to others who have also been affected by the setback. You won't be any good to your constituents if you are reeling from the effects of the setback and feeling profoundly discouraged. On the other hand, don't be afraid to show some vulnerability: you're human, after all, and you can receive support from the people you lead as well as offering support to them.

Once you are prepared emotionally, it's important to learn from the experience. While the temptation may be to put a setback behind you as quickly as possible, don't do it too quickly, or you are likely to encounter a similar situation in the future. Try to be as objective and dispassionate as possible in evaluating what happened. Avoid personalizing. "She's a nasty person" is less helpful for learning than "She hadn't completely bought in to our vision." There is not much you can do about someone's personality, but if you conclude that someone wasn't as aligned with your aims as you anticipated, you can take many kinds of actions in the future to increase the likelihood that the person will be more in sync. Maybe you'll want to do this after a contained period of venting. After all, we're only human!

Another way in which emotion can cloud a helpful assessment of what happened is by assigning blame. "I really screwed up. I am such a loser" does not offer insights for future successes. *I really screwed up*, *In what ways?*, and *What can I do differently next time?* is probably a more helpful set of questions.

After setbacks, as a way to collectively put things in perspective, it is sometimes helpful to review previous accomplishments. But not just from a cheerleading point of view. Instead, you can pay close attention to why those situations worked and what was different about this one.

Ultimately, it's helpful to remind yourself of the quote by Ron Heifetz: "Leadership requires the courage to face failure daily."[24] The truth is, if you are really exercising leadership, you are hanging out in uncharted territory a lot of the time. Why wouldn't there be setbacks?

"As a result of exercising leadership, I just experienced a huge loss."

In chapter 2, we explored the reality that leadership is risky. Taking on leadership roles opens one up to all sorts of consequences. As leaders, we regularly risk being criticized or blamed by others, being isolated from our peers. We can even risk loss of employment if we take a stand on an unpopular issue in the workplace. Parents of people with disabilities also risk the well-being of their children if they tackle problems with the services being delivered. One mother recently mentioned that she was afraid her nondisabled children would be adversely affected if she was too vocal in the school attended by her disabled child.

The risks are real, and no matter how well prepared we think we are, we can be caught off guard when something bad happens as a consequence of our leadership. Years ago, I helped to organize a conference where the keynote speaker was a psychiatrist named Thomas Szasz. At that time, Dr. Szasz was known as the "anti-psychiatry doctor," because he held the position that mental illness was a myth—in other words, that there was no biological basis for the conditions termed "mental illness." As a result of working on that conference, I came under personal attack by a chapter of the Alliance for the Mentally Ill, an organization that held dramatically different views about the causes of mental illness from those of the doctor. Members of this group even attempted to have me fired from my job. The director of the agency where I worked at the time was admirable in her unwillingness to give in to the pressure, and I retained my job. But I remember that my first reaction was, "What did I do wrong? I'm just trying to do the right thing." In my mind, I knew that having such a controversial speaker was risky, but the actual consequences were totally unanticipated.

Before you assume a leadership role on a particular issue, it can be helpful to do an inventory. Consider the potential risks, how well prepared you are for their happening, what allies you have, and what other strategies you can employ to minimize the chances that the risks will be realized. Keep in mind that in spite of this kind of thoughtful planning, it's easy to be caught off guard when consequences do occur.

When something does happen, you might be tempted to say, "Forget it. It's just not worth it." And that may be so. But like many of the recommendations in this chapter, the first thing to do is take a step back. Give yourself some breathing room to see if you can get some perspective. Check in with your deeply held values and beliefs. Is the work in alignment with your core values? If so, perhaps the costs are bearable. What would be the consequences of giving up this work? Most of us are willing to live with numerous costs in order to live in a way that is consistent with our core beliefs. It can also be helpful to review the stories of people who stood by their commitments even when difficult things happened to them—as a reminder and a source of inspiration.

In this chapter, I have tried to address some common questions and concerns that arise in the course of exercising leadership. Perhaps you have another concern or question. If so, feel free to contact me; I'd be happy to address it. And who knows? Maybe someone else had the same question.

CHAPTER 6
THE LEADERSHIP PRACTICE
OF SELF-AWARENESS

INTRODUCTION

The next few chapters will explore some core practices of leadership and offer a set of tools for strengthening your ability to apply each practice in everyday life. One of my favorite quotes is from Richard Carlson: "You become what you practice most."[25] It can also serve as a disturbing wake-up call, especially when my behavior is inconsistent with my values.

The practices addressed in these chapters require deliberate actions and structures that enable them to become habitual. Leaders don't just sit around waiting for some monumental leadership challenge to land in their lap someday and then expect to handle it beautifully. You really need to practice all the time, using the many opportunities presented in everyday life.

SELF-AWARENESS: THE FOUNDATION OF LEADERSHIP

The first and foundational practice of leadership is self-awareness. Have you ever been in a situation where you acted thoughtlessly or reflexively, only to regret your actions later? Most human beings can answer yes to that question. When you are in a leadership role, the potential fallout is much greater, because you have more influence than in other situations. The impact of your actions is magnified, and thus your responsibility to strive for self-awareness is greater.

What is self-awareness? I would describe it as the ongoing monitoring of one's internal states as those states interact with conditions in the outside world. Self-awareness is informed by reflection and learning from previous experiences. For example, you might have discovered that when someone uses a particular word—fill in your "hot button" word; we all have them—you literally see red. You may or may not know why that is so, and the original reason may no longer be relevant. You are not in a position to go back in time and change the experience that associates such strong emotions with that word, but you can monitor your responses to that word in the present time. By being aware of your habitual response to certain kinds of stimuli, you create opportunities to choose how you wish to respond, thus increasing your skillfulness as a leader.

Let's do a little exercise, focusing on your personal "hot button" words, which can also be phrases, body gestures, or even looks.

1. List a few words that really get to you. Or perhaps it's eye-rolling, finger-pointing, and so on.
2. Pick one of these—the one that has the most "charge."
3. Describe the past three times this occurred in your company and what your response was (feeling, behavior).
4. Would you describe your responses as skillful or unskillful? In what ways?
5. If unskillful, what would be your ideal response the next time this happened in your presence?
6. What will you have to do in order for this response to occur? Some people I've coached have come up with strategies such as laughing, taking a deep breath, even walking away. Others have found that merely noticing that they are starting to get hooked served to keep them grounded.

This exercise is a small example of self-awareness. It involves paying attention, learning from your experiences, and then using the learning to guide your future actions. I once listened to an audio book in which the author said, "Between action and reaction there is always a moment of choice." It sounds like so much common sense, but it involves a lifetime of attentiveness. Being able to simply notice the moment of choice might be a big first step, even if you fail to act as skillfully as you'd like in the beginning.

What other areas of life might benefit from self-awareness? We have already noted how we respond to certain "hot buttons"—words, body language, gestures, tones of voice, "looks"—or their absence. Many people have a strong reaction to being ignored or not being properly acknowledged in some way.

Self-awareness also involves paying attention to what conditions bring out your best and what conditions make it likely that you will be at your worst. Some people come alive under pressure and respond to a tight deadline by doing their best work. Others crumble. Some people can function perfectly well on four hours of sleep a night; for others, four hours would leave them mentally fuzzy and grumpy. Although we cannot always control these circumstances, it makes sense to aim for the most ideal conditions, especially when the stakes are high. It's also helpful to pay attention to behavior that seems self-defeating, like staying up late to watch a football game the night before an important job interview or picking a fight with your significant other just before a stressful meeting.

Self-awareness is an important discipline in other areas of life as well:

- Energy level: Are you a high-energy person? Do you like as much activity as possible, or does that overwhelm you? Are there times of day when you are at your best and other times when you can barely think a coherent thought?
- Work habits: Do you like to multitask and/or work on a variety of activities in small chunks of time? Or would you rather focus on one thing in depth for a period of time?
- Physical health: What contributes to your physical health or illness?
- Your internal monologues or stories: These are the stories you tell yourself about why something happened, what is likely to happen, why someone behaved the way they did, and so on. These are often so familiar to us that they become unconscious, and yet they have enormous power over our perceptions and our actions. What stories do you tell yourself, and how do these stories impact your sense of well-being?
- Your response to certain kinds of people, those of a particular age, gender, ethnic background, level of education, occupation, and so on: Are you intimidated by the prospect of talking with a group of teenagers? Executives? Men? Do you enjoy being in the company of working-class people? Quilters? Engineers?
- Your orientation to conflict: Do you "love a good fight"? Or are you more likely to be hiding somewhere if voices are raised?
- Values and deepest commitments, loyalties and alliances: Not only is it important to be aware of what these are, but it's also important to be aware of whether you are behaving consistently with your values or you're out of alignment. Additionally, knowing when your values conflict with someone else's can

give you valuable information about the relationship, yourself, and the other person.

How does self-awareness relate to the work of leadership? First of all, one aim of self-awareness is to create conditions that bring out your best whenever possible, thus creating a ripple effect with those you interact with. When I feel relaxed, rested, and adequately (but not excessively) challenged, I am able to focus on the well-being of others. When the opposite conditions prevail, I tend to pull inward, protecting some part of myself, and am consequently less available to create conditions that bring out the best in others.

Self-awareness also allows us to compensate for our limitations, thus increasing our potential skillfulness as a leader. If you are unaware that working with certain kinds of people makes you feel uncomfortable, then you might not consider the option of working with a partner in order to create the best possible result. If you are unaware that conflict causes you great distress, you might find yourself trying to "smooth ruffled feathers" instead of bringing in a facilitator who can surface the potentially constructive conflict that is simmering below the surface. A very effective strategy is to team up with other people to compensate for our limitations, or to avoid potentially unconstructive situations entirely, and to figure out another way to accomplish the work of leadership. If we lack self-awareness, these strategies will be less available to us.

In addition, self-awareness provides us with data that helps us be aware of how we are similar to and different from others. This is critically important to our success at "giving work back to the people." It may seem simplistic, but often what gets us into trouble is assuming that because we are a certain way, everyone else is too. Because we like tight deadlines, our colleagues will be overjoyed to have an eleventh-hour project to complete. Because we feel comfortable around top leaders, the other members of our group will relish the chance to meet with them. Understanding that people really *are* different can increase the chances of operating skillfully as a leader. You'll be able to work with people starting from where they are, rather than assuming that your preferences are shared by everyone.

Finally, self-awareness relates to the work of leadership in regard to identifying adaptive challenges. Earlier I wrote that a key principle for identifying adaptive challenges is to be able to take a bird's-eye view. It's not attached to a particular position or perspective but rather focuses on the greater good. When one is too tied to a particular point of view, it is difficult to identify an adaptive challenge. It takes a great deal of self-awareness to know our own biases and assumptions, to set them aside, and to examine what might be the greater good and not what *we* believe would be best.

CULTIVATING SELF-AWARENESS

There are many approaches to cultivating self-awareness and many helpful books and programs. Here, I would like to briefly describe a few options and possibilities.

One approach is to find a teacher, mentor, or guide. This can take many forms, depending on your orientation. Seeking out the guidance of a spiritual teacher from one of the faith traditions is a long-recognized path to greater self-awareness. This often involves participating in a spiritual community and adopting practices particular to that community, such as meditation or prayer. Finding a coach or a therapist is another approach to mentoring, as is seeking the guidance of someone you respect—perhaps a family member.

Soliciting feedback from others can also cultivate greater self-awareness and can be very helpful, since we often do not have reliable information about how others perceive us. Keep in mind, though, that you are learning about yourself through the filter of others' mind-sets; try to get feedback from a range of people without putting too much weight on any one response. Don't forget to do your own check-in! Only you know what's going on inside you. The Buddhist nun, Pema Chödrön writes, "The main thing about ... all practice ... is that you're the only one who knows what is opening and what is closing down; you're the only one who knows ... everybody else [is] giving you their feedback and opinions (which is worth listening to; there's some truth in what people say), but the principal witness is yourself."[26]

Be careful of soliciting too much feedback from others. Especially at first, it can be painful and challenging to take in. It's easy to blame the messenger and/or reinforce negative perceptions of yourself. Structured forms of feedback, such as 360-degree feedback, where the responses are anonymous and there is debriefing with an experienced coach, can be very constructive.

Another approach to cultivating self-awareness involves becoming more aware of our own mind-sets, also known as *mental models*. What do I mean by "mental model"? These are essentially the "maps" we carry in our heads about how the world is. These maps can be extremely useful in enabling us to sort through massive amounts of information and stimulus that we are exposed to. They allow us to quickly size up situations and take action. As such, mental models are extremely adaptive. The problem comes when we start to think of our mental models as the whole of reality and to believe that everyone views reality in exactly the same way. This single fallacy—that everyone views reality in exactly the same way—is at the root of much miscommunication and disagreement. We all have our own unique sets of mental models that are formed as a result of numerous influences, such as our upbringing, our cultural background, our religion, our personality type, and previous experiences. Becoming more aware of these and how they influence the way we perceive and interpret what we observe is an enormous contribution to self-awareness. One useful tool for becoming more conscious of our mental models is called the Ladder of Inference. This tool, developed by Chris Argyris, enables us to become more aware of the increasingly abstract sequence of thoughts that lead from observable data to conclusions to actions. This sequence can happen in an instant, often without our conscious awareness.

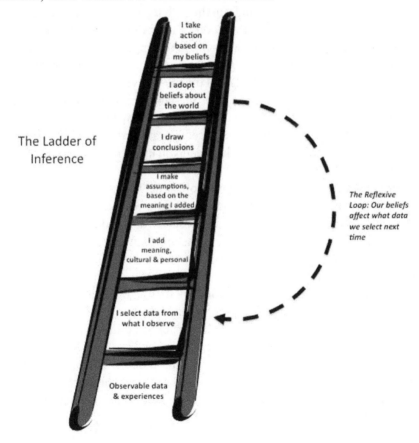

The Ladder of Inference

I take action based on my beliefs

I adopt beliefs about the world

I draw conclusions

I make assumptions, based on the meaning I added

I add meaning, cultural & personal

I select data from what I observe

Observable data & experiences

The Reflexive Loop: Our beliefs affect what data we select next time

There are limitless examples of the Ladder of Inference at work. Here's a simple one: You walk down the hall in your office building. One of your colleagues passes you, going in the opposite direction. She has a scowl on her face, avoids eye contact, and does not greet you as usual. This is at least some of the observable data; certainly it's the data you've selected. The meaning you add is that her body language indicates anger, because in your experience, people who scowl and avoid eye contact are angry. You make the assumption that her anger is directed at you and draw the conclusion that her behavior is a result of the argument you and she had at the staff meeting yesterday. This confirms your belief that you should never contradict anyone publicly, because that results in arguments that strain relationships. This belief then leads to your *current* action of avoiding your colleague because you don't want to further strain the relationship—and your *future* action of not speaking up at staff meetings.

Now let's rewind the tape and run through the Ladder of Inference with an alternate set of thoughts: You walk down the hall in your office building. One of your colleagues passes you, going in the opposite direction. She has a scowl on her face and does not greet you as usual. That's the observable data. But is it all the observable data? Perhaps you've already selected data from what you observed. Did you hear the phone ring in her office down the hall? Did you hear her exchange of loud words with the person on the other end of the phone and how she closed her office door a bit louder than usual? Would the addition of that data lead you up a different ladder? Very possibly.

But let's say it was only when your colleague was in your direct field of view that you started paying attention to the data you were selecting. Let's say you started noticing that you tend to select data, add meaning, draw conclusions, and take action—all in an instant. You stay aware that this is going on and realize that the only way to check out your assumptions is to interact with other people. So you see your colleague headed down the hall and you greet her: "Hey, Jane, you look distracted. Is there something wrong?" That gives her the chance to clarify what her body language signified—from her point of view. "Oh, I'm sorry. I didn't even notice you. I just got some bad news, and I'm mulling it over."

I have found that an awareness of mental models, combined with an ongoing practice to make them more explicit, contributes dramatically to self-awareness and to increased effectiveness in communicating with other people.

There are other ways to increase self-awareness. Personality tests, such as the Myers Briggs Type Indicator (MBTI) or Temperament, can increase awareness of your tendencies and preferences. These can be particularly useful in highlighting differences between people without the judgment that often accompanies our recognition of differences. Do you get energy by being focused on the outside world, or do you like to "go within" for renewal? Neither of these tendencies is right or wrong, and yet we often assume that there is something wrong with other people if they are not "like us." Or sometimes we think there is something wrong with us!

For example, when I was growing up, my friends used to come to my house and invite me to play with them. I would often decline, preferring instead to stay in and read. I always felt guilty and different. As an adult, when my husband and I go to the beach, he loves to walk around and talk with other people at the beach. He teases me because I'd rather stay under the umbrella and read a book, keeping to myself. When I took the MBTI, I discovered that my preferred approach to self-renewal is to spend time alone. Based on my husband's behavior, I have concluded that he gains energy by focusing on the external world and engaging with other people. Neither of these is the only "right way" to self-renew.

Keeping a journal is another way to cultivate self-awareness. There are many forms of journal-writing, and you can find guidance from many sources. There are dream journals, journals for stimulating creativity, grief journals, spiritual journals, career development journals, you name it. I recently did an internet search using the word "journaling" and found 7,160,000 references in .21 seconds!

I have regularly kept a journal since I was fourteen years old. While the form has changed over the years, my journal has been my companion and confidant through the ups and downs of my life. In my basement storage room, I have several boxes that contain every journal I have ever written. At some points in my life, I've gone back and read sections to try to make sense of the patterns of my life over time. My journal helped me understand that the seeds of my first marriage's breakup were planted at the very beginning of the relationship, and it helped me to forgive myself and my first husband and move on. More recently, I've used my journal to record creative ideas, business plans, and physical concerns, as well as to note relevant world events. I also write about the weather, family, and relationship issues. I write almost every day first thing in the morning, even when I'm traveling. Even though it's sometimes only one page, I don't feel the day has properly started if I am not able to write. These days, the journal serves as my idea and event memory. I can look back to a year ago and be reminded of what was happening in my life and in the world around me. Although not everyone is interested in journaling, it is a powerful vehicle for cultivating self-awareness.

Most areas of self-awareness that we have identified thus far are of the mental, emotional, or spiritual kind. Physical self-awareness is an area to pay attention to as well. Whether it's through yoga, martial arts, massage, or other practices, we can learn a great deal about ourselves through our physical being. Caroline Myss, a leading voice in the fields of energy medicine and human consciousness, asserts that "biography becomes biology." In *Anatomy of the Spirit*, she writes, "Every thought you have had has traveled through your biological system and activated a physiological response ... all our thoughts, regardless of their content, first enter our system as energy. Those that carry emotional, mental, psychological, or spiritual energy produce biological responses that are then stored in our cellular memory. In this way our biographies are woven into our biological systems, gradually, slowly, every day."[27] What a powerful idea! Most of us are vaguely aware of the mind-body connection. We know that our daily stresses tend to accumulate in one area of our back, for example. We know that certain experiences make us sick to our stomach. We know that some events provoke the "fight or flight" response. But contemplate the possibility that every thought we have leaves irreversible physical deposits. For me, the implication is twofold: I can learn a great deal about my thoughts by paying attention to what's going on in my body. But more importantly, I must consider the possibility that my physical well-being goes beyond exercising and eating right; it also extends to my thoughts. And when I have hurtful thoughts about a person or situation, even if I never utter a word, there is an irreversible effect.

IMPEDIMENTS TO CULTIVATING SELF-AWARENESS

Despite the reasons to cultivate self-awareness and the numerous approaches available, there are also impediments. Defensiveness is a huge impediment to self-awareness. In fact, defensiveness is a good clue that something could benefit from further exploration. Defensiveness suggests that we have something we're trying to protect, some kind of vulnerability, or wound. Often, exploring that area can reveal that it is not so scary, not so wounded; it just is. By gently exploring what we have been defending, we can develop greater acceptance and even appreciation for those aspects of ourselves that we wish were different and even come to understand that every one of our strengths has a shadow side. For example, if you are a quick thinker, which is a real strength, you might be prone to forming conclusions with inadequate information. This potential weakness is something you can pay attention to and minimize its negative effects.

Another impediment to self-awareness is an unwillingness to take personal responsibility, instead seeing other people and circumstances as responsible for our behavior. This is the victim mind-set, a perspective that holds that one is powerless and lacking efficacy. Frankly, this mind-set is incompatible with exercising leadership, and thus it's one that deserves regular attention. We always have choices, even in the most dire of circumstances, even if it's only over our responses. When you feel like a victim, ask yourself, "What are the choices I might make in this situation?" Viktor Frankl's classic book, *Man's Search for Meaning*, describes his experiences as a concentration camp inmate and his psychotherapeutic method of finding a reason to live. Frankl, who was a Jewish Austrian psychiatrist, observed that many prisoners died when undergoing less hardship and suffering than those who survived. The survivors tended to be people who envisioned a future for themselves despite their present suffering, people who believed they had a meaning in life and did not surrender to despair. He developed a psychological treatment method called *logotherapy*. According to Frankl, logotherapy was about striving to find meaning in one's life as the primary force. Frankl would help patients improve their mental health by helping them to discover meaning in their lives.

This chapter primarily focuses on self-awareness as it relates to you as a leader. But when you serve in leadership roles, you will also find yourself supporting the self-awareness of others. That is, you may be in a position to give others feedback aimed at enhancing their self-awareness. Sometimes that feedback is sought by others, and other times it is necessary but not asked for. I have found that taking a nonjudgmental approach is perhaps the most successful way to offer feedback that gets "heard." If you are seen as an ally of the other person and genuinely interested in their well-being, the person is more likely to take your feedback to heart. One important principle that I try to live by is to "tell the truth with love." Another thing I've learned through experience as both the giver and recipient of such feedback is that timing is critical. You may be completely well-intentioned in offering relevant, just-in-time feedback, but if the timing is not right from the other person's point of view, you may never get another opportunity. This is where empathy is key. Ask yourself, "When would *I* be most receptive to hearing some challenging feedback that is designed to help me learn more about myself?"

Sometimes as a leader you have to work with people who are not at all interested in cultivating self-awareness. If this is the case, don't take their behavior or attitude personally; it's their issue, not yours. Practice compassion and try to keep the relationship alive. Maybe they will be more receptive in the future. If all else fails, avoid them and find ways to work around them.

This chapter has addressed a critical practice area for leaders: the cultivation of self-awareness. In the next chapter, we will explore another important area for leadership practice: systems thinking.

CHAPTER 7
SYSTEMS THINKING: SEE THE FOREST AND THE TREES

INTRODUCTION

In chapter 4 we explored Marge Piercy's poem, "The Seven of Pentacles." The poem describes:

- Connections between cause and effect: "If you tend them properly, then the plants flourish, but at their own internal clock."
- Connections between the seen and the unseen: "More than half a tree is spread out in the soil under your feet."
- Connections between the interior and the exterior: "Weave real connections, create real nodes, build real houses. Live a life you can endure: make love that is loving."

This is a wonderful introduction to *systems thinking*, which is often a complex topic to explore. Essentially, systems thinking involves seeing underlying patterns and interrelationships between things rather than seeing these things as unrelated and separate. We will come back to this description again, but first it might be helpful for you to have some examples of systems as we proceed. Here are some examples to get you started:

- A garden is a system. Just as in Piercy's poem, the various elements of the system exist in relationship to one another and work together to produce a result that is greater than any one element could produce on its own. The gardener, the sun, the water, the mulch, the plants, and the wildlife described in the poem each have a unique and crucial role to play in how the garden behaves.

- An automobile is a system with many subsystems. The engine is a critical element of the automobile, but it is also a system in and of itself; it can operate in or out of the car. There are other subsystems as well, such as the fuel system, the steering system, and the brakes.
- The human body is also a system with many subsystems. There is the heart, the nervous system, the blood system, the respiratory system, and so on. They all must be connected to the others and operating in sync in order for the whole to work as intended.
- And then there are social systems, such as religions, political parties, families, and so on.

Everywhere we look, systems exist, but we may be quite unconscious of their presence. Take a minute to jot down one system you can think of in each of the following areas of your life: work, home, community, family, and spiritual. As we continue to explore systems thinking, we will come back to some of these examples. For now, let's return to my description of systems thinking—seeing underlying patterns and interrelationships—and develop the idea more fully, particularly as it relates to our capacity to exercise leadership.

THREE SETS OF EYEGLASSES

Imagine three sets of eyeglasses, each allowing us to see and experience the world in a particular way. The first pair is Type E, which stands for Events. Type E glasses are very helpful for seeing things one event at a time as a series of disconnected incidents, just like a set of snapshots. Type E glasses enable us to fully experience everything that is happening, but their limitation is that we are restricted to reacting situationally, event by event, without the capacity to meaningfully link these events together.

The second pair is Type P—for Patterns. Type P glasses operate more as a movie, enabling us to see and learn from patterns over time. Wearing Type P glasses can aid in planning and anticipating rather than merely reacting to events. Although we can predict what's likely to happen based on previous experiences, our capacity to influence what's going to happen is limited when we only use this set of glasses.

The third pair of glasses is Type S, which stands for Structure. Structure is what's below the surface of events and patterns, causing those events and patterns to occur. Type S glasses are the "link" glasses that enable you to see the connection between things you may have thought of as isolated. There are many kinds of structures, both tangible and intangible. A building is a structure that results in certain kinds of interaction and behavior. Relationships among people are structures, such as a family, a committee, an organization, or a program-planning team. Policies, rules, and laws are other kinds of structures. Mental models, those often-unconscious ideas about how the world works (introduced in the previous chapter), are structures as well. Mental models often give rise to the tangible structures that are visible to us. For example, a building starts out as an idea in an architect's mind about how people might interact with one another. From that idea comes a blueprint for a physical environment that, once created, results in the behavior the architect envisioned. When we can see things at the level of structure, we have the potential to design and create the results we want. Good systems-thinkers are adept at seeing the world through each of the three kinds of glasses and choosing which lenses are most useful for the situation at hand.

Here is an illustration drawn from real life. A family had a daughter with significant disabilities who was served in a residential program operated by one agency and a day program operated by another agency. She received transportation services from yet a third organization. The daughter had many professionals controlling her life and little say over what happened to her. She had developed a number of what were labeled "behavior problems," some extremely serious. If you looked at the world with Type E glasses, you might only notice her "behavior problems" on an occurrence-by-occurrence basis. Over time, however, the family observed that the daughter behaved differently—in a positive way—when she was at home with them and when she had more to say over her day-to-day life. They were seeing her behavior over time as a pattern—using Type P glasses. At that point, they could only *predict* what might happen, not *influence* the pattern.

By looking at the situation with Type S glasses, they realized that the only way to influence these patterns was to control the money that funded the "slots" in the three programs that served her. As a result, the family negotiated with the funding body and was able to pool the money that had been used to provide three discrete services. The funds were then channeled through a local service provider. The family used the money to help the daughter design what supports she wanted and needed. Over time, the daughter went from "someone who had no control over her life and severe challenges to someone who was making choices, being happy, and discovering her talents" (to quote her father). In other words, as a result of using systems thinking, they were able to create a structure that produced the desired results.

If the family had only viewed their daughter's situation through Type E lenses and focused on the behavior problems, their response would most likely have been very different. They might have tried to change her behavior through medication and/or through the application of behavior programs. While these responses could have been a necessary part of an overall intervention, they would have been insufficient and might even have made the situation worse.

I hope the example above demonstrates why systems thinking is an important discipline of leadership. Being able to think systemically increases the likelihood that you will be able to identify and address root causes and not just symptoms. This can minimize unintended consequences by keeping the focus on possible effects of an action over time, rather than simply looking at the present moment. Seeing things systemically is critical to identifying adaptive challenges and staying focused on the desired future, two important aspects of the work of leadership.

Unfortunately, systems thinking is a discipline that does not come easily to everyone. Partly, that's because it involves complex reasoning. But lest you be intimidated, let me say that in my experience some people without a lot of formal education are natural systems thinkers and grasp this way of looking at the world more easily than some highly educated people do. My theory is that our education works against thinking systemically. We are taught to think in terms of polarities: right and wrong, good and bad, cause and effect. The subjects taught in school are sliced and diced into tiny segments, with no holistic view. We study a country's geography separate from its history. We learn about ancient history and modern history as if they have no relation to one another. It was a revelation to me when I realized that the Holocaust had happened just decades earlier; when I was in school it was presented as if it were ancient history! Perhaps education has changed in the direction of supporting systems thinking; I certainly hope so.

In spite of all the obstacles to becoming a systems thinker, it is possible. You just need to practice. Here are some tools you can play with in order to increase your facility with systems thinking.

LEVELS OF PERSPECTIVE FRAMEWORK

Remember the Type E, Type P, and Type S glasses? Being able to see all three ways of viewing the world can tremendously increase your capacity to think systemically. There is a tool called the Levels of Perspective

Framework that helps encourage this kind of thinking by asking you to first describe an event of interest to you, then identify the patterns of behavior you've observed over time related to that event. Finally, you are asked to create a hypothesis of the structure(s) and possible mental models that you believe have caused the patterns and the events.

Here are several scenarios. What we are trying to do is apply the Levels of Perspective Framework in order to use systems thinking to understand the current situation. Then we can decide if we want anything to change, and use systems thinking again to help us figure out what change has the greatest likelihood of producing the results we are seeking.

Event	Low turnout at a particular family support meeting.
Pattern	During the past twelve months, attendance has been consistent for three months, drops off on the fourth month, picks up again for two months, then repeats the cycle.
Structure	Financial and administrative business takes up a large part of the meeting every three months. After a meeting with sparse attendance, organizers try new approaches to increase attendance.
Mental Model	"We have to conduct the official business during the meeting; there's no other way to do it." Or "It's always been this way."

Event	Signed up for an exercise program
Pattern	Always sign up in early January, start out strong but stop going by about April.
Structure	Trying to go it alone, live too far from the gym, family at home demands time and attention.
Mental Model	"Fitness is something you get to do after your real priorities." Or, "I should be able to sustain my commitment through willpower alone." Or, "My family is my first priority."

Event	Late to work
Pattern	Always late to work on Thursday
Structure	Wednesday night is softball and hanging out at the local sports bar.
Mental Model	"I work hard and I deserve to get a break once in awhile."

TRACKING BEHAVIOR OVER TIME

An understanding of how systems work can be aided considerably by paying attention to changes over time. Let's say that there is something you are interested in understanding more fully from a systems perspective. Let's use the family support meeting described above as an example. If you view what's going on at one point in time only (at the level of event), you don't have enough information to develop a hypothesis about the cause of the low turnout every few months. If, however, you look at turnout over a period of six months to a year, you can identify trends. But just looking at one aspect of this, such as attendance, isn't enough to get a sense of what is going on. You also need to identify other elements in this system (the "family support meeting" system). An element is *anything with a pattern whose behavior can be tracked over time.* In this example, attendance is an obvious element. Another less obvious element might be the amount of time devoted to business or administration during each meeting. A third element might be the various strategies used to influence meeting attendance—such as sending out additional notices, calling people the night before the meeting, offering stipends for people to attend, etc. We would want to track each of these strategies separately in order to determine what effect, if any, each was having on the system. Let's pick just one of those strategies in order to keep things simple: stipends. You could then draw some simple "Behavior over Time" charts of each of the elements we're tracking. For example:

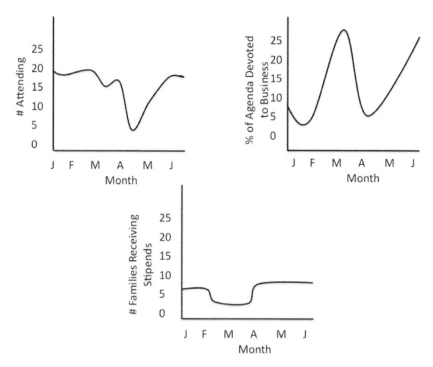

With these simple drawings, you may begin to notice connections between aspects of your system that you didn't realize were related. This allows you to form hypotheses and test them out to see if they explain anything about what's going on. If, for example, you notice that attendance goes down during the same month that the percentage of time devoted to business goes up, you then ask yourself, "Is there a connection? If so, what might it be?" One possible connection would be level of interest in the meeting content. You can then add level of interest as another variable and track that behavior over time.

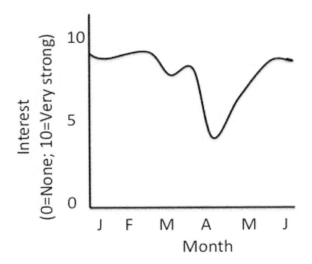

This gives you a much better chance to introduce an intervention that will make a positive difference. In this scenario, organizers try several new approaches designed to increase attendance. This might include making personal calls, changing the agenda, offering stipends, and so on. They know they are getting the result they want, but they don't know why. They may be wasting valuable time and money by making multiple changes if a simple change, like minimizing the percentage of the agenda devoted to business, would keep the attendance up. But they don't know that until they look closely at what is going on, the way we are doing here. According to the "Behavior over Time" diagrams, the stipends are making some difference but not enough to account for the dramatic fluctuations in attendance that seem associated with the amount of time devoted to business and administration.

TAKING SYSTEMS THINKING A STEP FURTHER

So far we have covered some of the basics of systems thinking, and there is much more that could be addressed. But I don't want to scare you off! Therefore, my plan is to take a couple more steps into the systems thinking forest by exploring how to do basic systems diagrams and laying out the main building blocks of systems thinking. There's much more to it than that, but you can follow up on your own if you're interested.

Remember that earlier I stated that much of our education works against systems thinking because it breaks things into little pieces and then examines those pieces as if they were completely separate. Systems thinking is the opposite of that: it is an approach that attempts to understand relationships, connections, and patterns in a holistic way. One tool to do this is through a systems diagram, also known as a causal loop diagram. Think of it as a kind of circular flow chart where each of the elements is linked to one another in order to visually depict the behavior of that system.

We've already identified an *element* as anything whose behavior can be tracked over time. A *link* is just an arrow connecting elements in order to describe the influence of one element on another. Let's go back to the family support meeting example. We've determined that the main elements we want to understand are attendance, level of interest in the meeting agenda, and how much time is devoted to business and administration. A simple causal loop diagram might look like this:

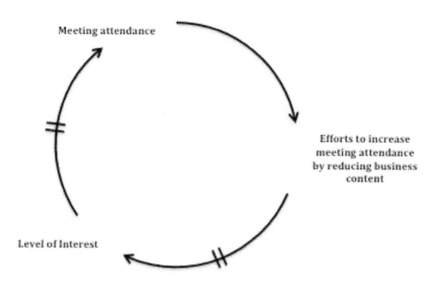

A description of this diagram might be: "Efforts to increase meeting attendance (by reducing business content) influences the level of interest, which influences meeting attendance, which in turn influences efforts to increase meeting attendance." This is why it is a causal loop diagram. A loop is basically a circle of causality in which every element influences and is influenced by another element.

So far we have not indicated anything about the nature of the influence, we have just indicated that the influence is there. It's very helpful to know if the influence is going in the same direction or in the opposite direction. Is it magnifying the next element or diminishing it?

Let's go back to the family support meeting. We've hypothesized that there is a connection between the three elements we are examining. We're pretty sure that as efforts to increase attendance (by reducing business content) go up, the level of interest goes up. As the level of interest goes up, attendance at meetings goes up. Are these influences occurring in the same direction or the opposite direction? That's right; they are the same. One element is magnifying the effect of the next one. As meeting attendance increases, what is likely to happen to our efforts to increase attendance? Mostly likely it will start to drop off as we reach our attendance goals. We may even start to slip back into our old ways of doing business. Thus the influence occurring between these two elements is in the opposite direction.

There is another concept that has significance for how systems behave: *delays.* What do we mean by this? Here's an example that's easy to imagine: It's early April, and you have just bought some pansies to plant in the planters on your deck. You want to have big beautiful pots of flowers on your deck by Memorial Day, but the pansies look pretty puny right now. In order to have a good showing, you put a mass of pansies into one planter and you sprinkle lots of time-release fertilizer into the soil. A week later, the pansies don't look much bigger, so you mix up some liquid fertilizer into the water as you're watering the pot and wait for the pansies to respond. Two weeks go by and they start looking a little fuller but nothing like what you are envisioning. Then you decide to have a party at your house two weeks before Memorial Day and your sense of urgency about these pansies increases dramatically. A little more fertilizer couldn't hurt them, could it? Three days later, instead of lush, full pansy plants, you've got sick-looking, blackened, misshapen foliage—and two days after that, all the plants mysteriously die.

Okay, so this is a bit of an exaggeration. Nobody would fertilize pansies that much. But it is a great example of the effect of delays on any system and of the consequences that can occur when we overlook or disregard the impact of delays.

Delays have a dramatic yet subtle impact on any system. Here are a couple of additional examples: Once I stayed at a retreat center that had an old and dispersed plumbing system. One morning, I turned on the water to take a shower. I waited at least two minutes, standing there in the cold, wrapped in a towel. The water was still freezing cold, so I turned it up. Time went on, water still cold, so I turned it up more. Impatient, I started showering in the tepid water, only to get a blast of scalding water shortly thereafter. I'm sure this has happened to many of us. And then, in response, we overcorrect and turn the water way down, so it becomes freezing cold again after a delay.

Delays are also at play whenever you introduce an intervention into a system. In the family support example, it might take several cycles of meeting before the intervention actually has the intended effect. In the meantime, you may not know whether your change is actually going to accomplish what you had hoped for. In the diagram on page 80, an anticipated delay is indicated by two hash marks. When looking at the diagram, the hash marks will remind you to be patient about the effects of an intervention.

SEEING YOURSELF IN THE SYSTEM

It can be easy to think of systems as something that exist "out there," as independent of us. This has the effect of discounting the impact we have on the systems with which we interact. As you are trying to understand a system, you want to ask yourself, "What part am I playing in how this system is operating?" It's not always apparent. For example, one of my colleagues told me that he had discouraged his wife and daughter from trying to fix things around the house, only to find that over time he ended up being responsible for all the "fix-it" chores around the house. Until he saw how his own behavior had influenced the system, he was irritated with his wife and daughter for putting that responsibility on him.

Here's another example that relates to a leadership situation. I was working with a team to address issues of accountability, personal responsibility, and meeting deadlines for a number of months. In initial conversations with the team leader and the company CEO, they both saw the team's problem as a skill deficit. We initially designed the engagement with that analysis in mind. Throughout the engagement, the team leader would routinely miss deadlines or complete tasks to which he had committed at the very last minute. Toward the end of the engagement, the team leader asked if he needed to complete a particular assignment that the team had agreed to do. When told that he did need to complete it, he then went four days past the due date before he attempted to complete the assignment. While he was frustrated that team members did not accept personal responsibility and meet deadlines, he did not see how his own behavior was influencing the system.

People in leadership roles probably have a disproportionate influence over the behavior of the system, yet they often discount their part in that system. Not only is leadership an element (patterns of behavior that can be tracked over time), but it is also a structure in that it *produces* patterns of behavior—just like funding, laws, the physical environment, and so on. Failing to see yourself in the system is thus a bigger problem when you're in a leadership role.

How to use systems thinking

By now you may be ready to move on to another leadership discipline, but let's finish up this chapter by exploring some of the applications of systems thinking. It's more than just a mental discipline; it is a whole way of seeing the world that increases the possibilities to influence the world in the direction of our vision. When one sees underlying patterns and structures, one has significantly more tools to influence the system in the direction of his vision, and in a more durable way.

Systems thinking is also an excellent way to describe the current state of a system without judging. Even dysfunctional systems are working for a purpose. Often those of us involved in change efforts overlook the fact that all systems are functioning the way they are intended to function, they just may not be functioning the way we want them to. When we are stuck in a cycle of poor choices, whether it is about taking care of our body or relationships that cause us pain, we benefit by taking the time to understand the system as it is currently operating in order to identify potential leverage points for change. If we don't do that, we run the risk of inadvertently thwarting our best change efforts. This is true with large systems change as well. Unless we understand the system as it currently is operating, we have little hope of initiating significant change, no matter how well-meaning the players.

Systems thinking is also a very useful way of identifying where there are human choices involved and where the elements are linked in a way that is "set in stone." When there are human choices involved that flow from particular mental models, we can become conscious of those mental models and then decide to make different choices. When the elements are tightly linked, we have less freedom to influence the result. Having this kind of clarity helps to focus on potential interventions that have the greatest likelihood of having the desired impact.

And finally, systems thinking provides a way of forecasting the future, allowing us to lay out several alternative scenarios and anticipate the potential consequences or effects of each. As such, it's a tremendously useful tool for leaders.

CHAPTER 8
CREATIVITY IS NOT THE SAME
AS BEING ARTISTIC

INTRODUCTION

Some years ago, I was teaching a three-day leadership program. We were exploring the topic of "time," and I asked participants to use crayons to draw a picture of how they envisioned their relationship with time. The crayons were set out in advance in front of each person's place, along with sheets of construction paper. As people entered the room, they groaned and made half-serious jokes: "I failed art in school," "I'm not the creative type," "I was really bad at coloring inside the lines," and so on.

This is the response many people give when the topic of creativity is raised. Is that your immediate response? Do you think of creativity as synonymous with *artistic*? As something outside your capability, even if you practiced and practiced? In this chapter, it is my intent to offer another way to think about creativity and to make the argument that creativity is an important discipline of leadership. I also want to share some of the conditions that limit creativity as well as some tools for creative thinking that work for many people, even those who don't think of themselves as creative.

WHAT IS CREATIVITY?

The term *out-of-the-box thinking* is used so frequently that it has become a cliché. Do you even know where the term originated? I discovered that it came from solutions to the so-called Nine Dot Problem where there are three rows of three dots and the problem is to connect all the dots with just four lines."

If you've never done the exercise, try it now.

Without lifting your pencil from the paper, draw exactly four straight, connected lines that will go through all nine dots but through each dot only once.

Hint: After you have tried two different ways, ask yourself what restrictions you have set for yourself in solving this problem.

Perhaps you discovered that the solution lies in drawing a line that goes outside the imaginary "box" formed by those nine dots. "Thinking out of the box" has come to mean thinking of a brand new solution that is outside of the bounds of what you already know and do.

Did you find a solution? It doesn't really matter; the value in this exercise is to gain insight into the assumptions we hold about how to solve this problem. To use the language introduced in chapter 7, thinking "out of the box" involves increasing awareness of our own mental models and deciding consciously whether these are helping or harming our ability to arrive at a desirable response to something we face. In the context of leadership, that is what I mean by creativity. (By the way, turn to the end of this chapter to see the solution to this puzzle depicted visually.)

CREATIVITY AS A KEY LEADERSHIP PRACTICE

A July, 2010, article in *Newsweek* focused on creativity—in particular, research indicating that American creativity is waning and what the consequences and solutions might be. The article cited a poll of 1,500 CEOs who identified creativity as the number one "leadership competency" of the future.[28] Creativity is absolutely essential in addressing the complex challenges we confront as individuals, families, communities, and whole societies. Think about the previous chapter on the work of leadership, where "identifying the adaptive challenge" was considered one of the fundamental things leaders do. Creativity is a core capacity that enables leaders to do this effectively. Creativity plays a part in identifying the adaptive challenge at several points.

First, creativity allows you to examine a situation and to become conscious of the tacit rules constraining your choice of responses. Some possible constraints include, "It's always been done this way," "We could never do that," or "There's no way we'll get away with it." That's not to say that those rules are wrong or inappropriate. But the initial step in leading creatively is to become more conscious of what those rules have been up until now.

Here's an example from my own experience as a quilter. I went to visit a wonderful quilt shop owned by a woman well known for her original and colorful quilts. I had only made one or two small art quilts under the tutelage of an accomplished quilter who had great technical proficiency and precision. My first attempts at quilting using a technique called "watercolor quilting" were visually pleasing from a distance; colorful, but not particularly precise. My seams were slightly irregular and the corners of my squares did not meet exactly, producing a rather wavy effect that, once pieced together, needed to be squared up by cutting off slices of all four edges.

I looked at the books on quilting technique and asked the owner of the shop to recommend a basic quilting book. She asked me, "What are you interested in doing?" I replied that I wanted to do art quilts, but I felt I needed to get the basics down, like precision piecing. (For nonquilters, this is where you take small pieces of fabric—squares and triangles and diamonds—and sew them together so the points and the corners join exactly. Precision has never been my strong suit, although I admire it.) She said, "If what you want to do is art, why would you care about precision piecing? Why not do what you enjoy?" Why indeed? Although I did purchase a book on quilting basics that day, I rarely refer to it. Instead, I've experimented with several approaches to quilting that use curved pieces of fabric, frayed fabrics, and other techniques that don't require precision. If the shop owner hadn't challenged my tacit assumptions about what the quilting "rules" were, I might be dutifully but miserably trying to do precision piecing (or might have given up quilting entirely!) Thus a first step in identifying an adaptive challenge is to become aware of the assumptions that frame our exploration of potential responses. Then we can consciously choose which of these assumptions or "rules" to leave in place and which need to be revised in order for us to move ahead with the work of leadership we have taken on.

An individual planning meeting, such as an Individual Educational Planning meeting, is a great opportunity to question the tacit "rules" and revise them to suit your leadership aims. Let's see if we can identify just a few of the unspoken rules that govern many of these kinds of meetings:

- The professionals are in charge. The meeting is held in their venue, it suits their schedule, and the agenda is set by them.
- Professionals are the experts.
- It is not acceptable to express strong emotions in such meetings. Strong emotions are considered a sign of weakness.
- Service recipients or their families need to be "armed" with as much knowledge about relevant laws and regulations, otherwise they will not get what they deserve.
- Service recipients and professionals are in an inherently adversarial relationship, often at odds over allocation of resources, time, or amount and type of service that will be delivered.

What if you decided that some or all of these rules did not serve your interests? That is exactly what many people receiving services and their families have done over the years in an effort to realign the relationships between people served, their families, and the professionals who serve them. The last rule, however, is one that I have rarely seen revised. Perhaps because people have experience being in an adversarial relationship so often that they cannot imagine another rule that might produce the result they want. Much of the legislation entitling people with disabilities to services is based on this rule, and so is the advocacy that is aimed at securing appropriate services. How different might both the process and the outcome be if the rule was, "We're in this together. We are in partnership toward enabling John to have the best life he possibly can"? With this as the rule, the adaptive challenge might be to ensure that all people get what they need and avoid the no-win, competitive battle that often seems to occur.

A second aspect to identifying the adaptive challenge that calls for creativity relates to systems thinking. It has to do with taking a broader view of a situation that confronts you, bringing in more elements than those you have initially thought were elements of the challenge, and exploring how those could be related. Here's one example: I was meeting with staff from several of the community agencies serving elders in Massachusetts. We were talking about the challenge of finding adequate numbers of qualified candidates for the position of case manager. One participant commented that she could not discern a pattern in the numbers of people who applied for a case manager position from month to month. She said the salary was the same, they used the same ad, and some months no one would apply while other months many people would apply. Since their agency is located in an industrial urban area, the group discussed whether a potential factor might be the closing or downsizing of other kinds of companies in the area. The participant thought that might be plausible and said she would look into it. If that turned out to be an element in their system, the agency could then be more proactive about recruiting workers from companies that had just closed or downsized. The creativity required in this situation was to expand the thinking about what factors might be contributing to the fluctuation in applicants and to look for possibilities outside of the system as initially defined.

Another way in which creativity helps to be able to identify an adaptive challenge is being able to envision a desired future. It's much easier to figure out what challenges you face if you're clear about where you want to end up. Envisioning a future that does not exist requires setting aside preconceived mind-sets in order to see what already exists in new ways—and then to extend what already exists into a whole new realm.

In addition to aiding leaders to identify adaptive challenges, creativity can also support them in uniting people with different or even opposing viewpoints. Using creativity to identify and question the tacit rules governing behavior can help identify areas of previously unrecognized common ground. A simple example: two parties disagree about a meeting date. One party is only willing to meet on a week day. The other party is only willing to meet on the weekend. The tacit rule is that the meeting occurs during the day, perhaps because it "always has." The application of creativity would say "Let's think outside the box here" and might identify alternative meeting times. This is a very simple example, but at its core lies an often-encountered impediment to finding common ground—the existence of unconscious rules and assumptions that limit people's choices. Once those are identified, much more freedom of choice emerges.

QUALITIES THAT SUPPORT THE EXERCISE
OF CREATIVE LEADERSHIP

Reflecting on what supports the exercise of creativity, I am reminded of a mother of three children with disabilities who has presented at a family leadership series for several years. Until recently, she came to the presentation highly prepared, her index cards neatly organized and her speech delivered in a compelling but controlled way. This time, she showed up with only the pictures of her family to prompt her. She hadn't had time to do the extensive preparations she had done previously. Her talk was powerful! It was funny; it was sad; it was touching; it was spellbinding. When she finished, she said, "Did I do all right? I was so unprepared this year!"

As this story illustrates, creative leadership can entail courage and risk-taking. This mother stepped out of her safe zone, the one in which she had presented herself in a controlled, moderated fashion. Instead, she showed the courage to reveal her pain, her desperation, and the depth of love for her family in an authentic way. Creative leadership involves wading into unknown messes and working with complicated relationships, passions, and differences as the medium for making progress on important issues—often with no precise idea what the outcome will be.

Being willing to live with an uncertain outcome is supported by the quality of curiosity. "Isn't that interesting? I never imagined things would go that way." "I wonder what's going to happen next?" It's like a dance with whatever comes up. That doesn't mean, as a leader, that you wade into situations unprepared. But it does mean that you cultivate the capacity to stay open and interested about what is presenting itself, and you stay willing to work with that.

How to cultivate creativity

So you're finally convinced that creativity is a key leadership capacity and not just a trait possessed by artists. But how do you strengthen your "creativity muscles"? Do you do exercises like the Nine Dot Problem on a daily basis? Actually, what you probably need to be doing is not practicing any one thing on a daily basis. In his article, "The Trouble with Out of the Box Thinking," Andrew Hargadon argues that, in order to cultivate creativity, we need to "find our discomfort zone." He writes, "The more comfortable we are in a particular setting, the less we need to think about what we're doing. The problem with being comfortable is that it means we're not challenging the existing norms of whatever group we're in. We're playing our role appropriately and competently. The problem is that it becomes difficult to try new things, think new thoughts, and pull ideas from the outside. By contrast, we tend to be most uncomfortable when we're working in new settings, where we're not quite sure what's the right thing to do or the appropriate way to behave, and we're not sure that we have anything to contribute. Those are the moments when we find out that indeed whatever this new situation is we've seen something in the past that might work. Whatever we come up with, chances are it will be different than what's been done before."[29]

Seeking out new opportunities and experiences is one way of placing ourselves in our discomfort zone (more on discomfort zones later), but there are also proven strategies and techniques to encourage creativity that require only that we mentally seek new connections.

Mind mapping is one such technique. Developed by Tony Buzan in the early 1970s, it was originally intended as a tool to help people take notes more effectively. In the course of its application, he discovered that it also contributed powerfully to students' thinking skills. I have used mind mapping for developing presentations, writing, note-taking, project organization, and in many other areas. Michael Gelb, a colleague of Buzan's, wrote, "The greatest power of mind mapping is that it trains your brain to see the whole picture and the details ... to integrate logic and imagination."[30] I strongly recommend that you practice this technique whenever you want to develop an idea or sort through an issue or problem. The more you practice, the more you will discover that you have ideas about topics you never thought you knew anything about. Here's how to do it.

1. Get a blank piece of paper that is 8 x 11 or larger—the larger the better!

2. Put a key word that you want to work with in an oval in the center of the paper. It may help to work in pencil initially, although later you may want to make connections using different-colored pencils or markers.

3. Now, begin to create branches to other ovals that are your main subjects. It may help to have the topics that seem to be closely related to your central concept as direct branches from that concept with less significant ideas that branch from those. But don't worry: there is no right or wrong way. The idea is to get the ideas flowing, not make judgments.

4. Write down every idea that comes to you, no matter how unrelated or insignificant it may seem. You never know where the idea might fit. Especially if you are trying to explore new territory, seemingly unrelated words and ideas might lead you to a new insight. Also, if you don't write everything down, you're likely to start judging and evaluating, which can block the flow of new ideas. There is always the opportunity to later discard something that doesn't work.

5. If you get stuck for ideas, keep your hand moving by drawing circles or doodles in the corner of the paper. I don't know why this works, but it does!

6. Once you feel you are done, you can use colored pencils or markers to cluster ideas that seem connected to one another.

7. Feel free to use visual symbols as a kind of shorthand. Some examples of common symbols are:

91

Up arrow—more, higher, increasing
Down arrow—less, fewer, decreasing
Right arrow—faster
Left arrow—slower
Exclamation point—excitement, definitely
Question mark—uncertainty
Asterisk—Important idea
You can also use clouds to indicate thoughts, smiley faces, rainbows, or any other symbols that work for you.

Try mind mapping each of the following: Your dream vacation, a special anniversary celebration, a work or volunteer project that you have been putting off, planning a meeting, writing an article, or organizing a presentation.

Mind mapping is one example of many tools aimed at improving thinking, especially a particular kind of thinking termed "design thinking" by creativity expert Edward de Bono. He contrasts this with "judgment thinking," both in process and in intent. *Judgment thinking* relies on logic, analysis, and linearity. *Design thinking* is about possibility, intuition, and leapfrogging from one seemingly unrelated idea to the next (also referred to as "lateral thinking"). Both have their place, but we get into trouble when we use one kind of thinking to serve a purpose that it is not suited for. In my writing, I used to try to compose and edit at the same time. Trying to combine *design* and *judgment* thinking is very ineffective, and it also results in distress. Have you ever had a conversation where one person asked, "Why don't we …?, What if we …?," and the other person immediately responded with the reasons why the idea would not work? How quickly did the person who was using design thinking give up, get angry, or become demoralized? In a sense, that was also happening with my writing until I learned to separate the composition (application of design thinking) from the editing (judgment thinking). Now my writing flows much more easily and is actually fun to do.

Skillful leadership, which is often about opening up possibilities and finding new and better ways to work together, requires the practice of design thinking. However, leaders also need to know when it's time to evaluate the soundness of new ideas and create plans for implementation that are actionable. This calls for judgment thinking. The creative process requires both types of thinking. Knowing when to apply which kind of thinking is key.

Hopefully, you are now convinced that creativity is an important leadership capability, and you have confidence that, with the help of some fun and easy-to-use tools, you can strengthen your creativity muscles.

Here's the answer to the Nine Dot Problem exercise:

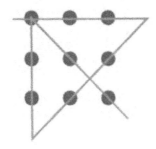

CHAPTER 9
COMMUNICATION: THE MEDIUM OF LEADERSHIP

INTRODUCTION

How does leadership actually happen? One significant way it happens is through communication. Communication is a key tool for creating shared vision, for mobilizing people, for organizing people to do their best work. Communication—or, rather, miscommunication—also causes most of the greatest difficulties in the work of leadership.

When we are in a leadership role, we must pay particular attention to communication. Not only must we be aware of how we ourselves communicate, but we must also consciously create "communication zones" that enable others to communicate effectively. Those are two important responsibilities of leaders.

The topic of communication is so rich that this chapter will focus primarily on oral communication that occurs day-to-day in the course of exercising leadership. Written communication, leading meetings, and delivering a presentation are other topics under the heading of communication. There are many other excellent resources available on each of these.

A COMMUNICATION MODEL

Here is a simple definition of communication: "Communication is the exchange and flow of information and ideas from one person to another. It involves a sender transmitting an idea to a receiver. Effective communication can occur only if the receiver understands the exact information or idea that the sender intended to transmit."[31] The key is *effective* communication. We all can describe many examples of communication gone awry; considering the number of factors that influence the communication process, it's no wonder. The chart below can be very useful in pinpointing the source of these communication snafus. We will only be able to improve communication when we know what got in the way.

Please bring to mind a communication snafu that you were a part of, either as the sender or the receiver. Jot down some notes on what happened, what went wrong, and what was the result. As you read through the descriptions of each aspect of the model, try to identify what contributed to your communication snafu and what you might do differently in the future.

Sender	Medium	Receiver
Mental Models • Experiences • Culture • Family • Gender • Religion • Personality Knowledge base Motivation Competencies	• Face to face • Email • Phone • 1:1/group • Oral • Visual *Message* • Clear thesis • Engaging format/structure • Credibility/authenticity	Mental Models • Experiences • Culture • Family • Gender • Religion • Personality Knowledge base Motivation Competencies

SENDER AND RECEIVER

Let's start by examining some of the factors that influence how the sender communicates and how the receiver receives the communication. Perhaps the most significant impact on communication are the mental models we each hold about every aspect of reality. You will remember that mental models are the "maps" that we carry in our head about how the world works. These "maps" are tremendously useful in enabling us to efficiently navigate a complex world, but they also create difficulties. When we assume that our own "maps" are like those of others—or that ours are the correct ones—we have created the likelihood of miscommunication.

Numerous factors influence our mental models. These include personal experiences, family and cultural background, and other influences in our environment. In addition, new findings in neuroscience have begun to reveal that there are physiological factors that influence our mental models, such as genetics and brain chemistry. For example, people who hold the "glass half full" mental model may actually differ in the makeup of their brain from those who hold the "glass half empty" mental model.

95

Whatever their origins, our mental models dramatically influence the communication process on both the sending and receiving ends. To illustrate, imagine someone who grew up in a large, gregarious household where the only way to get one's point across was to speak loudly and forcefully. This person communicates loudly and forcefully to someone who is timid by nature, one who also happened to grow up with a father who had a mercurial temper. The sender might hold the mental model that "the louder I speak, the more seriously she'll take what I have to say." The receiver might hold the mental model that "loud communication is a form of bullying" and be prepared to be abused. How do you think these different mental models might impact on their communication?

Another example: Let's say the sender has a mental model that the most effective communication is one with as much detail as possible. The receiver is a "big picture" kind of person who is not interested in detail. What might be the result of this kind of communication? The most innocuous result might be that the receiver is bored to death and can't wait to finish the conversation. A more problematic result might occur if the receiver interprets the sender's detailed account as reflecting the belief that he is incapable of thinking for himself.

The communication problems that arise out of unarticulated and differing mental models often snowball because it does not occur to the parties to question mental models. This often is due to the unconscious belief that our own mental models are the Truth. Thus, if someone interprets a communication differently, *they* must be in the wrong. Many communication snafus could be nipped in the bud if the parties stopped for a minute to surface their own mental models about the topic at hand. One of my clients routinely found herself in trouble in her organization because she held very tightly to the belief that her mental models were the "right ones" and dismissed the perspectives of others. Not surprisingly, her subordinates and colleagues found her to be arrogant and condescending. Only when she fully accepted the legitimacy of differing mental models— even those that were directly opposed to her own—was she able to begin improving her relationships in the organization.

Other factors that influence the communication that is sent and received include each party's knowledge base, their competencies, and their motivation. A sender who has a vast body of knowledge about the topic being communicated but who is unaware of the knowledge base of the receiver risks not being understood at all. That happens to many of us who find ourselves utilizing any kind of technical support, such as for our computers. The sender (the tech support person) often has a large base of knowledge about the topic, yet the receiver—us—rarely has such knowledge. As receiver, we may have to ask the technician to slow down, to repeat what they are telling us to do, or even to go back to basics—such as "How do I turn on the computer?". Or maybe we act like we understand what is being communicated but then hang up the phone and try to find a friend to help.

When the sender has a smaller knowledge base than the receiver, it can cause other problems, particularly for the sender. In this case, the nature of the communication may need to be adjusted to be more of an interaction; the role of the sender as "facilitator" rather than "expert" may also need to be established. Some of my coaching clients are leaders in technical areas where they lack the depth of knowledge of those they are leading. Trying to fake the knowledge is a recipe for disaster. Instead, a sender in this situation needs to establish a credible role for herself. A family member who is communicating with a doctor, for example, is in the legitimate role of advocate and from that role can communicate quite compellingly, even without an equivalent amount of knowledge in the medical field.

How competent is the sender at getting their point across? And how competent is the receiver at understanding exactly what was meant? This is another set of factors that influences how well the communication will go. Mastery of language can contribute to competency at both sending and receiving. Being able to use examples, metaphors, and analogies that are relevant to the receiver is another relevant competency. As sender, reading facial expressions and body language that indicate the receiver is "getting it" can increase the effectiveness of the communication.

On the receiving end, being able to concentrate and avoid being distracted is an important competency. If the receiver knows she/he is distractible, being aware of what conditions contribute to distraction is a useful piece of self-awareness. Being willing to ask questions and admit that one doesn't understand what is being communicated—or even to catch oneself when one's mind has wandered—can be powerful ways to increase comprehension of the communication.

Motivation of both the sender and the receiver is another factor influencing the communication. If neither party really cares, it's going to be difficult to engage in high-quality communication. At that point, the parties need to ask whether it's worth it. Maybe they need to find another time to have the conversation.

So far we've looked at characteristics of the sender and the receiver. Let's look at what's in between: the medium and the message.

The medium

There are many ways to communicate. Some are better than others for certain things. How the communication is received will be influenced by the *medium* that is selected, by the *context* (one-to-one or in a group), and by the *style*. For example, using e-mail to convey a message that has emotional or complex content is often a mistake. A phone call or a face-to-face meeting is much more effective. Even if you think an e-mail would be more efficient, if you have to spend hours compensating for a misunderstanding, you've lost whatever efficiency you may have gained (and you may have lost much more, such as goodwill or trust).

Communicating negative feedback to someone in a group setting is rarely effective. Again, you may think it saves time, but it also prevents a person from saving face and can have harmful repercussions for your relationship with that person and with other members of the group.

If your receiver is a visual person, drawing a picture or using a metaphor can be a good way to increase the likelihood of being understood.

These are just some examples of the impact a medium can have on communication.

The message

Finally, the message itself must be clear, have an engaging structure, and be credible in order to have the greatest impact.

One key strategy for increasing the *clarity* of communication is to recognize that the communication process starts way before something comes out of your mouth or is written on the page. It starts with how clear your thoughts are. Recently, a client complained that her team was not conforming to her expectations. I asked her if they knew what her expectations were. She said, "I didn't really know myself until now." How can we expect others to receive our communication clearly if we're not clear ourselves?

One of the most useful practices for increasing communication clarity is to challenge yourself to get your point across in thirty seconds or less, by focusing on your thesis or main point. Even if you are delivering a long presentation, having a thesis is critical and helps to focus your thinking.

Years ago, sometime during the mid-1980s, I was having dinner with two colleagues, one of whom was a teacher. At some point during the conversation—I don't remember the context—he made the statement, "When you open your mouth, your mind is on parade." I have never forgotten that statement! In fact, for months afterward, I was terribly self-conscious every time I uttered a sentence.

Do you have a messy mind? Are your thoughts strewn all over, like a closet that has not been cleaned in years? Or are they neatly lined up, sorted by color? It's not so important what the starting point is. What is important is that you discipline yourself to pull those thoughts together into a main point.

A former supervisor of mine gave me many opportunities to practice this skill. When I walked into his office with a problem or a situation that I wanted help sorting out, before I'd even start, he'd exhort me to "get to the essence." That focused me in a hurry!

Mind mapping can be a useful tool for surfacing your main thesis among the many thoughts you might have on a topic, thereby increasing clarity about the message you want to communicate. In chapter 8, I introduced mind mapping as a tool for increasing creativity. It can also be helpful to outline a presentation, memo, or letter you need to write.

Using the steps outlined in chapter 8, identify a message you need to communicate to another person and create a mind map. Then, before you lose the insights, write that memo or create an outline of that message.

We have focused on clarity as one key quality of the message. Next the message needs an engaging *structure*. Essentially, this is a format that allows the listener to maintain their attention and maximizes comprehension and flow. There are many types of structures to communicate a message. Some examples include:

- *Compare and contrast* ("The benefits of this course of action compared to the benefits of that course of action are as follows …")
- *Chronological* ("In 1999, a small group of parents with common interests joined together. The next year, they formed an organization. Two years after that, they applied for and received funding …")
- *Problem/solution* ("Despite many efforts to change the situation, people with disabilities are still lonely and isolated in community life. The solution to this problem would be to …")
- *Case study* (The case study uses a specific situation or vignette to raise broader questions and illustrate larger dynamics. Although there is not a set format, it usually involves describing a particular situation and then drawing implications or raising questions that arise from the case.)

The structure or format of a message is like its undergarments: meant to be invisible but supporting the message. It allows the receiver to relax and receive the content with minimal distraction and therefore to maintain attention and interest. You can use these structures to make a report at a meeting, write a letter, or organize a formal presentation.

Finally, for optimal impact, the message needs to be *credible*. The receiver needs to see the message as consistent with who the sender is. If you are delivering a message on behalf of someone else and you don't really believe in that message, the quality of the communication will be negatively affected. Even in those situations where you're only the messenger, it's important to find a way to communicate with authenticity.

Although this communication model is helpful, it is not comprehensive. There are many other factors that impact on the communication process. One of these is the *power* or *status relationship* between those who are communicating. This is an important thing to be aware of in the context of exercising leadership. Often people in leadership roles are unaware of the "magnification factor" that exists just because they are filling the role. Something that might have been communicated by a leader in a tentative way, such as an opinion or a request, can be magnified by others into a judgment or a demand.

Another factor that impacts on the communication process is *emotion*. Emotion can have an impact on communication; communication can also impact emotion. For example, a straightforward information transfer that is clogged by preexisting hurt feelings and anger is likely to go awry no matter how effective the sender or how clear the message. Conversely, the tone of the communication or the words that are used can serve to trigger the receiver, thus resulting in strong emotion, even though unintended by the sender. These are important considerations that have only been touched on here.

PRINCIPLES FOR EFFECTIVE COMMUNICATION

The following are a handful of core principles that, when consistently applied, enhance the quality of conversation.

BALANCE ADVOCACY WITH INQUIRY

One principle of skillful discussion proposed in *The Fifth Discipline Fieldbook* is that of "balancing advocacy with inquiry." What this means is that, in addition to trying to get our point across, we also curiously inquire about the perspectives of others. Stephen Covey has a related principle: "Seek first to understand, then to be understood." In the *7 Habits of Highly Successful People*, he writes, "If I were to summarize in one sentence the single most important principle I have learned in the field of interpersonal relations, it would be this: *Seek first to understand, then to be understood. This principle is the key to effective interpersonal communication.*"[32]

It can be exceedingly difficult to live by this principle. Often we simply lack self-discipline or self-awareness. We're used to saying whatever comes to mind without censoring or noticing what's going on with others. It takes conscious awareness to balance advocating our own point of view with listening to the perspectives of others—and being truly curious rather than merely asking as a courtesy. During a conversation, many of us are mentally rehearsing the next point we want to make while the other person is talking. When that happens, we are not really listening to the other person, and yet we expect they will listen to us! Pay attention to whether you're focused on what's going on in your own head or what the other person is saying. Make a commitment to try to increase the amount of the latter; I guarantee it will improve your communication.

HOLD YOUR OWN PERSPECTIVE LIGHTLY

We can easily become convinced that our own perspective is the right one or even the only one. This results in little interest in the views of others. In leadership roles this is deadly, because much of leadership is about mobilizing others, which involves paying attention to and considering their views. When you find yourself stuck in one perspective, it can be helpful to ask yourself, "What are some other ways of viewing this situation?" You can even be playful with it and use your favorite book or movie characters, animals, etc. Or you can think about someone you really respect and ask yourself, "How would she view this?" Of course the easiest way to remind yourself that there are multiple perspectives is to actually ask others—and then listen to what they have to say.

BE AWARE OF YOUR OWN TRIGGERS

In the chapter on self-awareness, we discussed "hot buttons," sometimes called *triggers*. Put simply, these are stimuli that set off our fight or flight response. Triggers can be statements, looks, or tones of voice that have the effect of overwhelming us emotionally. Often these triggers connect to an experience in the past and/or to something we deeply value or are protecting. As a consequence, we are catapulted into a less-than-skillful state of being that can take the form of literally fighting or fleeing. At the very least, it becomes very difficult to reason when we are in a triggered state, and thus our communication is unlikely to be very skillful. Once we become aware of our triggers, we can create space between stimulus and response, thus enabling us to choose our response rather than reacting.

Take a minute to write down all the words, phrases, tones of voice, or expressions that you know are triggers for you. (You may need more than one piece of paper. Until I did this exercise, I thought I was unflappable!) Pick one of these that really bothers you; make a commitment to becoming more aware of when you are triggered by this, and develop strategies for maintaining choice. Once you've made headway with this trigger, pick another one.

HAVING DIFFICULT CONVERSATIONS

Having difficult conversations is where the rubber meets the road in the communication arena. Of course, it's important to have a clear thesis, to get your point across, to be understood, and so on. But the art of communication comes in when there's something that needs to be discussed and it's going to be hard. Often such conversations have to do with deep issues of trust, accountability, and self-esteem. What makes them difficult is that they often arise from values clashes. For example, reliability is a strong value of mine. If I make a commitment, I will do whatever I can to follow through, and I hold that expectation of others. When others don't follow through, I'm faced with the prospect of having a difficult conversation. Many times the conversation goes well. When it does not, the relationship suffers, and I feel out of integrity.

Because these conversations are so hard, people often avoid having them. Yet many communication snafus arise precisely because people put them off. You feel like your spouse has consistently shirked her responsibilities on the home front, but you don't say anything because you don't want to rock the boat. You need to give someone hard feedback, but you don't say anything because you're afraid of hurting his feelings. You're unhappy with the quality of services your child is receiving, but you don't say anything because you fear repercussions. With each of these examples, there is an understandable reason for not initiating the conversation, but there are likely to be consequences as a result of holding back. In their book *The Relationship Cure*, John Gottman and Joan DeClaire write, "When things go wrong in a relationship, people often ask, 'Was it something that I said?' Well, maybe. But more often it's the things people *don't* say that harm their relationships. According to the psychologist Dan Wile, many arguments spring from issues that people need to discuss but never do. In the resulting tension and confusion, quarrels erupt, leading to hostility, defensiveness, and withdrawal."[33]

Here are some ideas to help you prepare for and engage in difficult conversations.

PREPARATION

It is worthwhile spending some time preparing before the conversation. Write out some of the history, background, and the context. Think through really carefully what you want to bring up. In *Crucial Confrontations*, the authors point out that difficult conversations are rarely simple. They write, "Problems rarely come in tiny boxes—certainly not the issues we care about. They come in giant bundles."[34] Therefore, it's helpful to be clear about what aspect of a situation you want to focus on. Let's say your teenaged son borrowed the car without your permission, went out drinking with his friends, and had a fender bender on the way home. You might be tempted to confront him with the whole thing and maybe that's exactly what you need to do. But first think through what you really want as a result of this conversation. From your perspective, what's the real issue here? And how do you want things to be?

Another way to get to the "what" of your conversation is to use the acronym *CPR*. The first time the issue comes up, focus on Content (C): describe just what happened at the level of event. The next time the issue comes up, focus on Pattern (P): What has been happening over time? As the problem continues, focus on Relationship (R): What is this doing to us? How is it impacting on our relationship? This approach uses a systems thinking perspective to help you determine what to focus on.

Another suggestion for determining your focus is to notice not only what happened but also the consequences and what you perceive to be another's intentions. In the example above, the actual consequences of your son's actions were relatively mild, but the potential consequences were enormous—particularly of drinking and driving. That may be what you want to focus on.

A further example may illustrate intent. Your daughter's teacher has made her stay late after school, and you believe the teacher dislikes your daughter and is out to get her. If this indeed was the teacher's intent, you might want to focus on that in conversation with the teacher, rather than on the fact that staying after school causes her to miss her bus. But be careful here when you try to discern another person's intent. Our own assumptions and mental models are very much at play here, and we may inaccurately assess another's intent based on our interpretation of their behavior.

As you continue your preparation, pay attention to why you believe this conversation is going to be difficult and what actual evidence you have that this will be the case. Often our expectation that a conversation is going to be difficult contributes to the difficulty because we feel tense, defensive, or angry. When we can approach a potentially difficult conversation with curiosity, openness, and no expectations, the emotional cloud that surrounds the conversation often dissipates.

Also, pay attention to the desired outcomes of this difficult conversation. Do you want to win? To get the other person to do what you want them to do? To have an open and honest dialogue? To feel that you've been heard and respected? Part of this reflection also involves considering whether you actually want to have the conversation at all. Perhaps you had a bad experience with someone that you will never have to interact with again. Is it really worth engaging in this difficult conversation? Or maybe you determine that the potential costs of speaking up are likely to be greater than the costs of keeping quiet. Keep in mind that we often overestimate the costs of speaking up in relation to the costs of keeping silent. Does your conscience keep bothering you but you have kept quiet until now because you're worried about the consequences? What is the cost of your silence?

Once you've decided what the conversation needs to be about and whether it's worth having, you might further reflect on who you want to be as you engage in this difficult conversation. What are you willing to take responsibility for? Rather than trying to control or change the other person's response, prepare yourself for how you want to show up in the interaction.

INITIATING THE CONVERSATION

Extensive preparation sets the stage for initiating the conversation in a way that has the greatest likelihood of going well. At the very least, you have done *your* part of the work. A further suggestion is to pay attention to how you actually want to bring things up. Thinking about what the context will be is a first step. If you want to talk to a staff person who serves your family member about the way he speaks to her, doing so in a neutral environment, one-on-one, might be helpful. But you also want to pay attention to the way you actually start the interaction. Gottman and Silver write about something they call the "harsh startup." "The most obvious indicator that this discussion ... is not going to go well is the way it begins."[35] A harsh startup involves sarcasm, criticism, judgments, complaints, and generalizations ("You always, you never"). They write that 96 percent of the time you can predict the outcome based on the first three minutes of a fifteen-minute conversation. They suggest starting with a positive statement, expressing appreciation, keeping it specific, and using "I" statements. If this is a person you have a really hard time being positive about, it helps to practice thinking positive thoughts and paying attention to what you appreciate about this person before you even have the conversation.

CONTINUING THE CONVERSATION

While there is much more that could be said about engaging in difficult conversations (see the bibliography for some great resources), here is one final tool that I have found tremendously helpful: "Yes, *and* ..." instead of "Yes, *but* ..." This is a tool that's drawn from improvisational theater. In essence the principle is that every time you are tempted to respond to something a person says with a "Yes, but ...," you practice saying "Yes, and ..." Then follow it up with something that builds on what the other person has said. For example, you've asked your daughter to clean her room, and she starts complaining that she doesn't have enough time because she has to finish her homework. Instead of responding, "Yes, *but* you still have to do both anyway" (What's the likely effect of that?), try something like, "Yes, *and* I really appreciate what a good student you are and how important good grades are for you." (What might be the effect of *that*?) The amazing thing about "Yes, *and* ..." is that it focuses your attention on what you have in common, on how the various perspectives build upon rather than negate one another, and ultimately that simple phrase has the potential to bring people closer together rather than to polarize them.

This has been an attempt to share with you some important tools for leaders in the area of communication. It has been by no means exhaustive. Hopefully, what has been covered will stimulate you to explore the area of communication in greater depth because, as we have seen, it is the medium of leadership.

CHAPTER 10
USING CONFLICT AS A CONSTRUCTIVE FORCE

INTRODUCTION

Webster's Dictionary defines *conflict* as "a clash, competition, or mutual interference of opposing or incompatible forces or qualities (as ideas, interests, wills): *antagonism*." Where, in the course of leading, are you likely to run into these situations? Heifetz and Linsky write, "When you tackle a tough issue in any group, rest assured there will be conflict, either palpable or latent. That's what makes a tough issue tough."[36] Whenever you take on a leadership role, you must be prepared to consider conflict to be part of the work.

I must confess that I tried to finish this book without writing a chapter on conflict. "Well," I told myself, "I've already addressed interpersonal conflict in the chapter on communication. Aren't there already plenty of books on conflict? What do I have to say on this topic, anyway?" And every time, something brings me back to the plain truth that it's unacceptable to write a primer on leadership without addressing the topic of conflict.

Conflict avoidance is something that is familiar to many of us. It's natural; it's part of our makeup as social animals to want to get along and cooperate. We see conflict as something scary and dangerous, where there will be winners and losers and nobody stays friends. But is that the mindset that's most helpful? How can we view conflict as a constructive force rather than as a scary, dangerous thing? That's what this chapter is about. In particular, the focus is on conflict in group contexts, although there may be occasional examples drawn from interpersonal conflict.

You might be asking yourself if *all* conflict needs to be addressed. Isn't it sometimes best to "agree to disagree"? Sure! Otherwise we'd be spending our lives locked in disagreements with others and focusing all our energy on addressing the disagreement. Some conflicts are just too insignificant to make them a priority. So here's my litmus test for taking on a conflict: Determine whether your group or team is blocked in its ability to make progress toward its vision by the presence of a latent or overt impasse. In those circumstances, it is critical to identify and address the conflict in order to proceed with your work. If you envision leadership as a journey toward a desired future, conflicts are like boulders sitting right in the middle of your path. Until you discover the nature of the conflict, you will continue to bump into that boulder over and over again until you collapse in exhaustion. You certainly will not be able to devise a set of strategies for addressing it.

IDENTIFYING A CONFLICT

It may seem odd, but it's not always easy to identify the presence of a conflict, especially if it's latent. Of course, we all can tell there's a conflict when people have raised their voices and are arguing. But what about situations where a group can't make progress on their goals no matter how hard they try? How is that a conflict? Latent conflicts are often harder to pinpoint and address than full-out arguments. They manifest in an unaccountable drain of energy and momentum, a lack of commitment and follow-through, or in gossiping and factionalism. Latent conflicts are sometimes referred to as "undiscussables" or "elephants in the middle of the room." These are topics perceived as so central and yet so sensitive that even to name them is to risk some horrible fate. Or so group members fear. And yet, not naming them often leaves the group stuck and unable to make lasting progress toward their vision.

Overt conflicts present their own challenges in identifying the topic. Often what people are arguing about is not at all what the conflict is *really* about. Remember the chapter on systems thinking where we talked about Events, Patterns, and Structures? Often people can be arguing at the level of Event ("You haven't yet repaid that loan I made a week ago"), when there's something else going on below the surface ("I'm always the giver in this relationship" or "I'm the primary breadwinner, and the division of labor doesn't seem fair"). Trying to see what's going on below the surface when emotions are strong and people are polarized can be very challenging.

Remember the acronym "CPR" (Content, Pattern, Relationship) that was presented in the chapter on communication? The first time an issue comes up, focus on Content (C) and describe just what happened at the level of event. The next time the issue comes up, focus on Pattern (P) and ask, "What has been happening over time?" As the problem continues, focus on Relationship (R) and ask, "What is this doing to us? How is it impacting on our relationship?" This can be one helpful way to identify the source or a conflict.

Let's do another exercise that can help identify the root cause of a conflict. It involves using a simple but powerful exercise called the "Five Whys." The exercise begins by identifying a situation you want to understand better and then asking yourself *why?* up to five times in order to arrive at a more fundamental understanding of the situation. For example, let's say I just had an argument with my sister while we were discussing our father's care. My inquiry might go like this:

> *Description of situation:* My sister and I had an argument the other day while we were discussing our father's care. She accused me of interrupting her.
>
> *Why?* I did interrupt her. I was in a hurry to get to work and was impatient with listening to every detail of what she was telling me. I wanted her just to tell me what the conclusion was.
>
> *Why?* (You could follow several paths at this point: Why was I in a hurry to get to work? Why was I impatient with hearing every detail? Why did I only want to hear the conclusion? Choose the path that you believe will lead you toward a deeper understanding.)
>
> *Why did I only want to hear the conclusion?* Because it's more clear-cut and less emotionally fraught. I prefer that.
>
> *Why?* Because I like to keep some distance from the messy details of family life. Aha! By realizing my part in this argument, I can then decide what to do about it with a more complete perspective. In this situation, I realized that my sister deserves to be able to share some of the details of what she's dealing with, since we're partners in caring for my father. I may prefer things to be clear-cut, but they aren't. I can't, in good conscience, leave the messy stuff to her. That realization lays the foundation for a follow-up discussion that's very different from what it might have been. In a few short "whys," you can go from a rather superficial description of the situation to something more fundamental, suggesting a fundamental way to address the situation.

Bring to mind a situation where a group of people do not see eye to eye. It could be something like planning a family holiday, where members of the family cannot agree on who will be the host. Or it could be the leadership group of an advocacy organization locked in disagreement over the focus of the organization's work this coming year. You might be involved in an overt conflict where there are raised voices and hurt feelings, or it could be latent, with no one talking about the situation and everyone acting as if things are fine—except that you're not getting anywhere.

Once you've thought of the situation, write a couple of sentences describing the conflict. Then, ask yourself a series of "why" questions: Why is it like this? Why is it like this? Why is it like this? Do this until you have a sense that you've gotten to the root cause of the conflict. If you have a couple of different scenarios, follow each of them to their possible root causes and see if one seems to ring true. Once you've done this exercise on your own, share it with someone else familiar with the situation to see what he or she might be able to add to your insights.

Keep in mind that, up until now, you have *not* considered solutions or ways to address this conflict. This is hard to keep from doing: we often want to jump immediately to solving the problem before we fully understand the nature of the conflict. But depending on the nature of the conflict, different responses are called for. Therefore, it's beneficial to spend some time trying to understand the nature of the conflict before considering solutions.

The Fifth Discipline Fieldbook describes four common sources of disagreement:

1. facts
2. methods
3. goals
4. values

This book suggests that "simply agreeing on the source of disagreement often allows people to learn more about the situation, clarify assumptions that previously were below awareness, and move forward."[37]

WHAT EFFECTIVE LEADERS DO TO ADDRESS CONFLICT

Leaders who are effective in conflict situations see conflict as an energizing force that often signifies important matters are at stake. There wouldn't be conflict if people didn't care! Such leaders approach conflict with curiosity ("What can emerge out of this?") and even excitement ("What can we learn from this experience? How can we capitalize on the energy that's present?"). But they take their leadership responsibilities seriously and understand that conflict handled poorly can result in longstanding and even permanent divisions and fractured relationships. When leaders find themselves in the midst of conflict situations, they will often do some of the following things.

CREATE A SAFE SPACE FOR NAMING AND ADDRESSING CONFLICT

The *physical* environment might be a place to start. What kind of physical space will members consider safe to explore a conflict? Perhaps it's someone's living room or a welcoming retreat center or maybe somewhere in nature. You might look for a physical space that is soothing and calming, rather than one that heightens tension and anxiety. Gently running water or calming music might be a helpful addition.

But there is also the *emotional* safe space that needs to be created. This can be done by engaging an experienced facilitator, if necessary. Another approach might be to create ground rules or techniques that participants agree will enhance their sense of safety (e.g., using only "I" statements, not "you" statements). If participants don't trust one another and are unwilling to raise issues publicly, having people anonymously write their concerns can be a starting point for open discussion.

If there are different "camps," encouraging people to mix up the seating can be a way to set the stage for a less polarized discussion. Also, having a table that people sit around can help or hurt the interaction. If people are feeling very tense, the presence of a table in between people can increase the comfort level; not having a table can increase the sense of intimacy between people.

UNDERSTAND THE ROOT CAUSE OF THE CONFLICT

As mentioned earlier, understanding what people are *really* in conflict over is a key to effectively addressing the conflict. Using a systems perspective can be very helpful to do this. The Five Whys exercise described earlier is one way to approach this understanding using systems thinking. To go into even more depth, try using the Event/Pattern/Structure/Mental Model (Level of Perspective Framework) that we explored in chapter 8:

1. Identify a conflict that is longstanding and troubling to you.
2. What's the story? (Events.)
3. What patterns have occurred over time?

4. How do you explain this? (Structure explains patterns and events.)
5. What mental models seem to contribute to the structures you've identified?
6. What would be a place to intervene in order to address this conflict?

As a leader, you can do this by yourself, but it's probably more effective to lead the parties through this together if the relationship allows for this kind of conversation.

HELP PEOPLE STAY FOCUSED ON THE VISION AND PURPOSE

When people run into impasses, they often shift their focus to the impasse and lose sight of the vision and their purpose for working toward that vision. It's like they run into a big boulder in the middle of the path, stub their toes, and then fixate on the pain. "Why me?" "This is just ruining my day!" Your job as a leader is to direct people's attention back to the vision (where they were headed before they ran into the boulder) and the purpose (why they were headed there in the first place). One team I coached would "stub their toes on the boulder" every time we got together. We'd be working away, making progress toward their vision, and then all of a sudden it was like the energy had been sucked out of the room. The first couple of times it happened, we spent a lot of time fixating on the pain: "What happened? This is awful! We need to (pick one) take a nap/go out for drinks/get some chocolate/find a new facilitator." The time after that, we just observed what had happened and that it seemed to be a pattern. From there on, we got more skillful. We said, "Where were we headed again? How can we get around this impasse to keep going?" Chances are, even if we'd been really skillful at the beginning, we would have needed a few toes stubbed to recognize the pattern and plan to address it.

Let's think about a situation where you might need to direct people's attention back to the vision and purpose. One example might be an ISP or IEP meeting. You're there as a parent advocate and you have a vision for your child. The professionals—speech therapists, physical therapists, teachers, aides, and so on—have their assessments and their own views about your child, and they aren't always completely in sync. If you wish to play a leadership role here, your job might be to direct people's attention back to a vision (preferably a shared vision) instead of bemoaning the fact that professionals are disagreeing among themselves. You might ask, "What are we here to accomplish together?" Having a common and compelling vision and purpose can help put conflicts into a larger perspective.

HELP PEOPLE IDENTIFY A WAY FORWARD

Once you've helped people to shift their focus from the effects of the impasse to their desired vision, you then need to help them identify a way forward. If the vision is the "where," then the way forward is the "how." Once you've reached an impasse, the "how" addresses ways to get beyond the impasse as well as ways to progress toward your vision. As mentioned earlier, this can sometimes be accomplished by getting clear on the source of the impasse, but not always. By the time things become conflicts, there are usually many thoughts, emotions, and experiences complicating the situation. This is where the real fun of leadership begins! Although there are no guaranteed strategies for success, some approaches are worth trying:

- Help the conflicting parties to identify and communicate their own mental models; create a framework for people to share those with one another.
- Help the conflicting parties to see things from the others' perspective. Even better, help the conflicting parties *experience* things from the others' perspective.
- Help people see their commonalities and focus on those. Rather than paying attention to the differences, look for what could unite people in moving forward.
- Pay attention to maintaining a sense of safety for all the parties. Understand people's needs and fears. The authors of *Crucial Confrontations* write, "At the foundation of every successful confrontation lies safety. When others feel frightened or nervous or otherwise unsafe, you can't talk about anything."[38] Whenever you sense that anyone has started to feel unsafe, they advise that you shift your focus to rebuilding safety and then return to finding a way forward once that's been repaired. Further, they propose that people feel unsafe when they believe either that they aren't being respected as a human being or that their goals are being disregarded. So, when you are in a leadership position trying to help people find a way forward, part of creating an atmosphere of safety is to consciously address those two considerations.

- Focus attention on issues, not personalities. Even when a group member has an abrasive personality, their views deserve to be understood and considered. It's often the role of the leader to direct people's attention to issues, especially when someone's personality gets in the way of a potentially valid idea. Also, while it's true that personality differences are sometimes the cause of the conflict, it's often worth exploring whether there are underlying differences that are masked by the difference in personality. Help people to look closely at the source of the conflict by examining differing mental models as well as differences in personality.

- Know when to let people save face. When people are in front of others, it can be difficult to concede. There's too much at stake. As a leader, you need to be sensitive to when it's necessary to back off, give people some breathing room and let them make up their minds without being pressured. A grudging concession is unlikely to produce the kind of commitment you want. And sometimes people are in the process of buying in, but they don't want to appear to have retreated from their original position. Be aware of these buy-in signs, and use them to the group's advantage—in a delicate way.

CONSIDER DISSENTING VIEWS

Sometimes conflict arises because a minority have strong views that dissent from the majority. It can be tempting to squash those views in the interest of continuing to make progress toward your vision. That's often not a good idea. If you shut down those views without giving them an airing, the people involved will be less invested in whatever is decided because they will feel like their perspectives have not been considered. If you do it forcefully or insensitively, people's sense of safety will be violated, and there will be even more harm done. And others will be afraid to speak up in the future. Besides, dissenting voices often have something considerable to contribute. As a leader, you want to encourage multiple perspectives and ideas, so it's important to find a way for those views to be aired.

AVOID GETTING SUCKED IN YOURSELF

When you are playing a leadership role, it's particularly important to avoid getting sucked into the conflict yourself. You will be rendered ineffective at everything you try if you do. Of course, that's easier said than done, particularly if you have strong opinions about the matter over which there is conflict. It can be helpful to think of yourself as wearing different "hats" to keep your role as a leader and as a group member clearly separated. If you know you have no chance of being objective in the situation, there's nothing wrong with turning things over to someone else or even bringing in someone who has no stake in the matter to facilitate the discussion.

PERSONAL PREPARATION FOR
LEADING THROUGH CONFLICT

In the chapter on self-awareness, we looked at triggers and mental models in some detail and explored how these affect our ability to interact and communicate with other people. We discussed techniques to become more aware of mental models and circumstances that trigger you. Clearly, this kind of self-awareness is critically important in conflict situations where the work of leadership is even more challenging than it is under less volatile conditions. Not only is self-awareness important under these conditions, but effective leadership also calls for *self-control.* Let's say you know that one of your triggers is to be called "stupid." Just knowing that is a start, but to function well in conflict situations, you also need to have developed the capacity to avoid reacting, even when triggered. Even better, you might eventually get to the point where you're not even triggered by that word, and you can respond in a calm and skillful way.

Along with self-awareness about triggers and mental models, it's helpful to be aware of your natural orientation to conflict, which interacts with previous life experiences that forged your beliefs about conflict. For example, if you grew up in a large, noisy household in which shouting at one another was the usual mode of interaction, you might have tried to avoid adding to the din by being quiet and "keeping the peace," as one of my clients recently acknowledged. Now that she is in a significant leadership position, she's discovering that her natural aversion to conflict is preventing her team from having the difficult discussions that are needed to move teamwork forward. Or you could have grown up in such a household and taken the opposite approach—that is, to be the loudest and most forceful voice. In leadership roles as an adult, you may be perplexed about why your people are reluctant to contradict you; you know you're not angry when you speak loudly, but they do not.

There are a number of useful inventories that give you a picture of your natural orientation to conflict. Perhaps the most well-known is the Thomas-Kilmann Conflict Mode Instrument (TKI), which has been in use since the 1970s. This instrument "uses two axes … called 'assertiveness' and 'cooperativeness' and identifies five different styles of conflict: Forcing (assertive, uncooperative), Avoiding (unassertive, uncooperative), Accommodating (unassertive, cooperative), Collaborating (assertive, cooperative), and Compromising (intermediate assertiveness and cooperativeness)."[39]

Even without using such an instrument, you probably already have a good idea of your natural inclinations regarding conflict. As a leader, you'll need to use your self-awareness as a starting point for expanding your range of responses to potential or actual conflict situations.

WHEN THINGS FALL APART

In spite of your best efforts to exercise skillful leadership in conflict situations, things sometimes do not work out smoothly. What do you do when things fall apart?

First, evaluate whether the parties absolutely must interact with one another in order to reach the goals that have been set. Sometimes, it makes most sense for people to go their separate ways. I once worked to organize a conference that brought together constituents who had fundamental differences of perspective about the causes of mental illness and what forms of treatment would be most helpful. The planning committee, which included people from the different constituencies, tried to reach common ground on an agenda and topics to be addressed during the conference. Throughout, there were heated arguments among members of the committee, which I attempted to mediate. Although we did piece together an agenda, there was never agreement among the parties. This resulted in a tense conference with open conflict among members of the audience. If I had been more experienced and less naïve at the time, I might have seen that these parties had irreconcilable differences that could not be bridged in order to plan and participate in a joint event. We might have been more successful if we'd held separate events that each addressed the same topic.

If there is significant difference but a need to work together, another approach worth trying is to create a way for people to interact at a distance. For example, if two members of a group can never see eye to eye but they each make valuable contributions, designate someone else as a go-between. Or have each person work on a different subgroup or committee. This is not ideal, but it can work, especially if the parties with the conflict agree on goals.

Sometimes it helps to take a break from trying to resolve the conflict, to get some breathing room in order for members to reflect on what's really important. You can even help shape how people think about this by inviting people to think of the shared purpose or history of the group, examples of successes working together, and so on. You might ask people to reflect on this question: "How can we turn this into a situation where everybody wins?" And finally, creating a framework that enables people to take the perspectives of others with whom they have differences can help bridge differences.

LINK TO OTHER DISCIPLINES AND PRACTICES

It's clear that self-awareness is a critical discipline for leading effectively through conflict situations. Systems thinking is another. If we see things systemically, we will have better tools to understand the root cause of the conflict. In addition, systems thinking supports the view that we are all interdependent and connected in some way and that what affects one part of the system affects the system as a whole. This view can provide real motivation for coming to a mutually acceptable resolution rather than letting conflict fester or sweeping it under the carpet. Applying creative, out-of-the-box solutions can also be a potent way of leading skillfully through conflict. Instead of sitting around a table and talking about a conflict, invite people to act it out, get up and dance, build something together, or take a walk through the woods. Who knows what the result will be!

CHAPTER 11
WORKING WITH TIME

OVERVIEW

Imagine this. You have finally managed to secure an appointment with someone you admire very much as a leader. You've waited months for this appointment because this person is in great demand. You're looking forward to talking with her, and you have several pressing matters that you wish to get her perspective on.

You arrive at her place of business, only to find a line of people outside her office, snaking down the hall. This is disconcerting and doesn't fit with your image of how such a leader would manage her commitments, but, after all, she is a busy person and very important. You take your place in the line. After an hour, you are first in line.

Finally, she ushers you into her office. She asks you to have a seat and then asks you to wait while she returns a "pressing phone call." You tell her you are happy to wait, and she proceeds to make the call.

Once that is complete, she asks you what you would like to talk with her about. Just as you are taking a breath to start, the phone rings. "Oh," she says, "I really need to take this. I'm waiting for confirmation of my trip next week."

The conversation proceeds in fits and starts, with people popping in, the phone ringing occasionally, and even beeps and pop-ups coming from her computer. Throughout your meeting, you feel as if you are a distraction, and you are never able to fully relax and concentrate—nor does she appear to.

As you leave, you reflect on your impression of this person, having actually met her. Your image of her as a leader of substance has been tarnished. Although she is unquestionably very much in demand, you do not feel you were personally attended to. Instead, you feel as if your concerns—and indeed your life—are one more task for her to manage in an overcommitted life. This interaction negatively impacts your impression of her as well as your sense of yourself.

Does this sound familiar? Perhaps you can identify with the leader— feeling overcommitted, overwhelmed, and desperately trying to offer some support, however insufficient, to the people who look to you for leadership. Or perhaps you are the follower, that person who seeks advice and support from an admired leader, only to feel diminished by an unsatisfying interaction. How we work with time has a considerable impact on the quality of our leadership.

WHAT'S YOUR RELATIONSHIP WITH TIME?

Before proceeding, let's take a little quiz about your relationship with time.

1. How many times a day do you say (or think): "If I wasn't so busy, I would …"? Make a list of all the things you would do.
2. Which of those things, if you accomplished them, would strengthen your capacity as a leader?
3. Finish this sentence: "Time is like a …" What does that suggest about your relationship with time?
4. List all the ways you regularly waste time. These can be important things—like not setting priorities and then running out of time to do what really matters. They can also be small things, like stopping to talk to everyone you know when you're trying to work out at the gym. What useful purposes do those "time-wasters" serve? (Suggestions: They make you feel important, keep you distracted from your problems, help you avoid doing what you don't want to do, maintain ongoing relationships.)

Once you complete this little quiz, please reflect on what might be some lessons about your relationship with time and your role as a leader.

I'd like to share an insight I had about my own relationship with time. One of my mantras is: "I'm so busy." In spite of the fact that this is almost completely my own doing, I still experience a considerable amount of stress as a result. Yet efforts to change have been unsuccessful. One day I was telling a colleague about a professional goal that is important to me. She observed that it seemed like a big, important goal and perhaps a bit of a stretch. When I reflected on that, I responded that it was not as much of a stretch as it seemed because I already had connections with people who could help move toward the goal. This person asked, "Why haven't you been in touch with them?" My answer? You guessed it: "I'm too busy." Too busy to take a step in the direction of an important dream. That really took me aback. What was I filling my time with, if not important dreams? Eventually, I realized that I needed to let some things go in order to fill my time with the realization of important dreams. Underneath that, though, was another layer, and that was *fear*! The things I was filling my time with were things I felt comfortable with, that weren't a stretch. Letting those go was like giving up a safety net. But then I realized that I'd been meandering in the direction of my dreams as if I had all the time in the world, and that not achieving my dreams might have an effect not only on myself but on the lives of others. No time to waste! This enhanced sense of urgency began to produce changes in the way I spent my time.

Working with time in a skillful way is a crucial discipline of leadership. Not only does your skill in this area impact your own life, but it also impacts the lives of those who look to you for leadership, as the opening vignette illustrates. Keep in mind that your behavior sets an example for others, whether it is your family, members of a group you lead, or the people who report to you. If you are habitually late, others will emulate you. If you default on deadlines, people will learn that deadlines are just suggestions. The tone you set while in a leadership role is one that will eventually influence how people behave in the arenas where you are leading.

Additionally, when you are in a leadership role, your priorities—and the clarity with which you communicate them—will have an impact on how other people use their time. If you are not clear, there will be confusion, duplication of effort, and eventually frustration and the inability to work toward your "desired future." In *Monday Morning Leadership*, David Cottrell sums this up succinctly: "One of the 'main things' for a leader is to eliminate confusion."[40]

Energy over Time

There's one other concept that I'd like to introduce before going into more detail about various tools, strategies, and challenges related to setting priorities and working with time. This is the concept of *energy* management rather than *time* management. The concept is very simple: Energy, not time, is the foundation of high performance. In their book, *The Power of Full Engagement*, Loehr and Schwartz write, "Leaders are stewards of organizational energy—in companies, organizations, and even in families.

They inspire or demoralize others, first by how effectively they manage their own energy and next by how well they mobilize, focus, invest, and renew the collective energy of those they lead. The skillful management of energy, individually and organizationally, makes possible something that we call full engagement."[41]

One practice that is critical to sustaining energy is *recovery*. In every arena, be it growing crops or training athletes, the secret to maintaining and improving performance is to build in periods of recovery at regular intervals. That is the only way to build muscle, to grow robust crops, or to maintain emotional and spiritual balance. Are you one of those people whose motto is "I'll rest when I'm done"? I used to be that kind of person, and I would work until I was exhausted (not to mention resentful, cranky, and ineffective). Since I have started paying attention to energy management, I take short breaks during the day, stop doing what I'm doing when I start getting grumpy or sloppy (if I have the choice), and maintain the practice of eating numerous small meals during the course of the day. I've also started creating practices that maintain a positive attitude and shift a negative mind-set to a positive one. These small but important changes have had positive results in terms of regulating my energy and attitude during the course of a day. If you are thinking, "Isn't she lucky that she has a lifestyle that allows for this," keep in mind that athletes such as tennis players have recovery routines they practice *between points*, a period of between sixteen and twenty seconds! And one of my coaching clients, who has a high-level position in the federal government, wrote me that although he considers himself to tend toward negative thinking, "I always benefit from the drill of *forcing* myself to think like an optimist when faced with an ugly situation, and it always generates a better attitude and even new approaches." Later in the chapter, we'll come back to some practices you might consider adopting to quickly facilitate recovery.

SETTING PRIORITIES

Let's start with the basic fact that every one of us has exactly the same amount of time available in the course of a day, a week, a month, and a year. What varies is what fills up that time. Granted, some of what fills up our time is not of our choosing. As a parent of a child with disabilities, you may have chosen to be a parent, but you didn't choose the additional challenges and responsibilities that come as a result of the disability. Even so, we all have much more influence over the ways in which we allocate our time than we usually acknowledge. When it comes to time, many of us see ourselves as victims. Before we even talk about setting priorities, we must shift our mind-set from being a reactive to a proactive person. One of the best ways to do this is to engage in a thoughtful process of priority-setting that links together your vision, your life purpose, your core values, and your goals and objectives. I call this *alignment.*

When we are in alignment, we are in a much better position to be proactive, to initiate actions that lead toward our vision rather than waiting for something to happen to us. We are also better able to come to a *choice* rather than thinking of ourselves as a victim. Once we have clarity about our own purpose and priorities, we can think about the ways in which these interact with the purpose and priorities of others in our family, our community, and our workplace.

Please pull out the work you've done on your vision statement. You will be further developing this by writing a purpose statement and starting to identify your core values. From there, you can develop goals that are consistent with your core values and your purpose, goals that direct you toward your vision. Once these are developed, it can be helpful to put them all together on one page or perhaps a laminated card that you can pull out and consult when you are making a decision or choosing a course of action. That way, your daily actions will be in alignment with your overall life plan.

PURPOSE AND CORE VALUES

I believe every person has a unique role to play during their time on earth. Whether we use the term *purpose, mission,* or *calling,* the idea is the same. It's the answer to the questions: *Who are we put on this earth to be?* and *How do we best use our gifts and talents?*

It may not be at all clear to us what our purpose is. We may have spent our lives trying to measure up to others' expectations while ignoring or submerging our own inner stirrings. We may never have been supported or encouraged to develop our gifts or to think of ourselves as even having something to contribute. Or we may have lived in such dire circumstances that the development of our unique identity was never a consideration.

In order to be in alignment, having a clear purpose is important. It's a crucial link between vision and goals: What is my own personal contribution to making the world the kind of place I have envisioned?

Over the years, I've tried out a variety of exercises designed to uncover one's own sense of purpose. This is an approach that works with many people:

1. Find someone to share this with or write a description of the following: Think of a time in your life that stands out in a positive way, a time when you felt like you were fully being yourself, "in your power." Perhaps it was as a parent, a community leader, or an employee. What were the circumstances? What about this experience was important to you? What gifts, talents, and contributions did you bring to the situation?

2. If you are doing this with a partner, have that person first listen to what you are describing and then share back some key words that stood out for them. Some examples of common words include "contribute," "teamwork," "family." Have your partner write those words down.

3. If you are doing this alone, write a few paragraphs that describe the situation, then go do something else for a while. Come back later and notice what words stand out for you. Write them down.

4. Whether you wrote the words yourself or your partner wrote the words, make sure the words are the most accurate and precise ones that describe what was important to you about that experience. Often, this is a good beginning list of core values.

5. You might add a few more by answering the question, "What else do I value that's not already written down?"

6. From your story and your list of core values, complete the following phrases:
    My purpose (as a leader, a parent, in life) is:
    To be or do (the action):
    In a way that (the quality of the action):
    So that (end result, outcome, the point of the action):

You may want to create a draft, set it aside for a few days, and then fine-tune the wording later.

I have used this sequence with many people, including people attending a workshop who were standing in front of a roomful of people as they composed their purpose statement. There is something powerful about linking purpose and values to a real experience where you felt very aligned. Thanks to fellow coach and colleague Heidi Sparkes Guber for sharing this format for creating a purpose statement.

This purpose statement format can be used for other things as well. You can use it to create purposes for organizations, for training events, even for phone calls and meetings. When you have such a purpose statement, the level of engagement goes up for even the most mundane activities. For example, once I was driving to conduct a focus group with direct-care staff who worked with elders in their homes. I was gathering information to find out what kinds of training needs these workers could benefit from. I'd already done about half a dozen of these focus groups; the drive was long, it was early in the morning, and the weather was gloomy. My level of engagement was not high, and I knew I needed to be more enthusiastic. So I created a purpose statement. It read something like this:

> *To* gather information from case managers on their training needs
> *In a way that* is fun, participative, and informative to all
> *So that* my parents and other elders living in the community will receive high-quality care.

Immediately, my sense of purpose and thus my engagement increased enormously, because now the meeting was linked to something I *really* cared about. I was also able to use this at the end to evaluate how successfully the meeting had gone, getting input from the focus group participants.

ARTICULATE YOUR CORE VALUES

Once you have created a purpose statement and an initial list of core values, see if you want to add more. Here are some examples of what people often come up with: fairness, justice, kindness, achievement, independence, loyalty, honesty, family, intelligence, etc. Write each value as an action statement—for example, "Be honest," "Love my family," etc. Write a paragraph of clarification under each statement. Some people include quotes; others use a definition of the key words. Whatever has meaning to you will work. Prioritize your list. This can be a difficult exercise, but it contributes to clarity in goal- and priority-setting. For example, if Love My Family is #1 and Acquire Great Wealth is #2, then you are likely to use your time and energy very differently than if the priorities were switched.

Be honest with yourself. Evaluate your behavior over the past few weeks or months; bring your behavior in line with your core values. Or if you find that you are consistently not living them, ask yourself whether it is truly a value you hold or if it comes from someone or someplace else. Many of us have "shoulds" that come from our family, our church, or other influences, but we don't own them enough to guide our behavior.

GOAL SETTING

The next step is to identify long range and intermediate life goals. It is helpful to consider each of the following areas: spiritual, social, cultural/intellectual, physical/recreational, financial, and professional.

There are a number of excellent planning tools available. I have used a system called *TimePower* by Charles Hobbs. Stephen Covey's work is also very useful. The Coaches Training Institute has a powerful exercise called "The Wheel of Life," where you first evaluate, on a scale of one to ten, how satisfying your life is currently in a number of life areas. You then create a visual depiction, using the image of a wheel, of how "well-rounded" your life is at the present. Then you are asked to envision the absolute ideal—a ten—and create goals to realize that ideal in the life areas that are highest priority. Whatever planning tool you use, the important thing is to make sure your vision, purpose, values, and goals are aligned with one another. This helps a great deal with setting priorities and managing time.

WHAT TO DO WHEN YOU'RE FEELING LIKE A VICTIM

In *The 7 Habits of Highly Effective People*, Stephen Covey introduces a framework called "Circle of Concern/Circle of Influence" that I often use with my clients and in my own life. I've adapted his work as follows:

1. Draw a big circle on a piece of paper with a smaller circle inside that. Label the big circle "Circle of Concern" and the smaller circle "Circle of Influence."
2. Identify as many things as possible that you care about, things that are on your mind. It could be global warming, your children's future, caring for your aging parents, issues or concerns at work. Write these in the outer circle, the Circle of Concern.
3. Next, pick one of those topics and identify an action or strategy you are already doing to address that concern. Write what you are doing in your Circle of Influence. Do that with a second concern.
4. Now, pick another one of the topics that you placed in your Circle of Concern, one that you are doing something about but not as much as your values would suggest you should be doing. For example, perhaps you have acquired several of those cloth grocery bags as a way to contribute to a sustainable environment, but your conscience has been nagging at you to do

something more. (Try to distinguish between your conscience and the "should" voice!) Think of an action that would be the next step in terms of having an influence over this concern by asking yourself, "What's the next action?" This question, although simple, is often challenging to answer. "Learn more about sustainability" isn't exactly an action; it's more of a project that has many action steps. "Research sustainability on the Internet" is somewhat more specific, but what is the intended outcome of your research? If your intention is to find an organization to join or to gather facts that you can use to influence others, then make that your action. Once you have an action in mind, write that in your Circle of Influence.

5. Finally, pick a concern that you feel really stuck on. It matters a lot to you, and yet you do not yet see a way to be proactive on this concern. Asking yourself, "What's the next action?," identify one concrete action that will move you from concern to influence, no matter how small. Write it in your Circle of Influence.

6. Celebrate! It's hard work to move from feeling like a victim to being a proactive person.

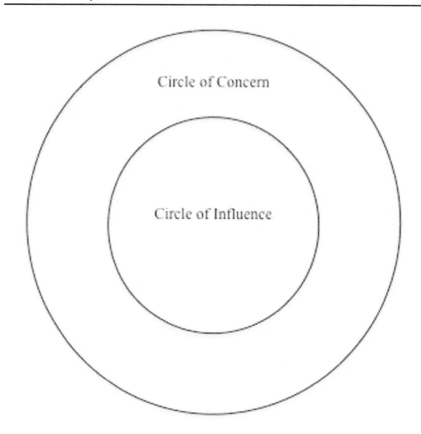

Circle of Concern

Circle of Influence

Covey writes that proactive people focus their efforts in the Circle of Influence. They work on the things they can do something about. The nature of their energy is positive, enlarging, and magnifying, causing their Circle of Influence to expand. Reactive people focus their attention on their Circle of Concern. They focus on other people's failings, global problems that seem overwhelming, or circumstances over which they have no control. This results in blaming and accusing, reactive language, and feeling like a victim. Focusing too much on your Circle of Concern without clarity about what concrete actions you are willing to take causes your Circle of Influence shrink. The exercise you just did is a way of strengthening your proactivity muscles. If you keep working with these Circles, eventually your Circle of Influence will expand considerably.

What did this exercise suggest about setting priorities? For me, what really stands out is how much time and energy I regularly squander on thoughts, emotions, and actions that are not within my Circle of Influence, and how little impact that has on what really matters to me. Conversely, when I am not clear about my priorities, I can find myself dwelling on things within my Circle of Concern without any goals or intention to act. Both of these tendencies perpetuate the perception that I am a person to whom things happen rather than an agent of action in my own life. Having clarity about our Circle of Influence is a very useful way to get out of the mind-set of "victim."

PRACTICAL STRATEGIES FOR WORKING WITH TIME

Now that you are clear on your vision, purpose, values, goals, and the next actions you will take to address those items in your Circle of Influence, will your life just run smoothly forever? Not a chance. As we know, even the best-planned lives encounter unexpected challenges along the way. This section will offer some suggestions for tackling those challenges in a way that enables you to experience time as a resource and not as an enemy to be fought against.

ADDRESSING COMPETING PRIORITIES

You may find yourself in a situation with multiple commitments that clamor for attention and seem to compete with one another. Perhaps you are committed to being the leader of a family support group, and you are also committed to having a rich family life. Both are important; each seems to be crying out for attention during the same time period. How do you address that and still keep your sanity? It can help to first bring to your awareness which of your values is reflected in each commitment. For example, leading a family support group might reflect the value "give back to others." Having a rich family life might reflect the value "put my family first." Once you've explored what values are reflected in each commitment, a couple of approaches are helpful. You can use your prioritized list of values as a guide to determine which priority takes precedence. For example, if "family" is your number one value and "service to others" is number three, you have a clue about how to prioritize that block of time. You can make a choice based on your higher value. Or you might ask yourself if there are ways of maximizing each of those important values, perhaps by enlisting family members to participate in the support group so you spend time with your family *and* provide service to others. Another way to think about this is over a span of time. I may be able to quilt, paint, garden, make a living, stay in good physical shape, and contribute to my community over the course of my life, but when I try to do all those at once, that's when I become overwhelmed. Which of these priorities am I willing to defer in order to have a manageable life?

127

Another strategy is delegation. If keeping a tidy home reflects your value of "order" or of "beauty," is there someone to whom you can delegate that responsibility? You might even consider paying someone to clean your house or bartering with a friend who is willing to clean your house in exchange for something she needs help with. The point is, you are choosing which of your priorities—and thus your values—to honor by how you spend your time. If this choice happens unconsciously or is dictated entirely by others, you're not using time in a skillful way to further your leadership commitments.

VALUE HOW YOU SPEND YOUR TIME

In *Meditation XVII,* John Donne wrote, "No man is an Island, entire of itself; every man is a piece of the Continent, a part of the main." As much as we might wish to pursue our own priorities and manage our time as it suits us, real life requires that we must coordinate our time and our priorities with others—often *many* others. As a result, all too often we become victims of the needs and priorities of other people. This leaves us feeling stressed, overwhelmed, and often resentful. How can we balance being proactive about pursuing what's important to us while being flexible about responding to the needs and priorities of others?

Here again, the first step is to truly believe that our own time and priorities are as important as those of others. *Truly believe!* This is not an intellectual exercise! How often do you reflexively defer to others' needs or their claims on your time? Or if you don't, do you go around feeling guilty, worrying that someone will think you're not a good person, that you're selfish, uncooperative, demanding? These thoughts and feelings create emotional baggage instead of a straightforward negotiation about how things might be worked out. A small personal example: I was working to arrange an evening conference call with a colleague. I proposed a time that worked for me because it enabled me to go to my regular dance class and get home in time for the call. The other person proposed that we talk an hour earlier—right in the middle of my class—so she could go to church. Until recently, I would have deferred to her, thinking her needs were more important than mine, or that church was more important than dance class. This time I said to myself, "We each have important priorities that we are trying to honor. Neither of them is more important than the other. Is there a way we can honor both?" And by compromising, we were able to arrive at a time that worked for both of us.

The key thing is that these small, everyday negotiations with others accumulate to become a life of honoring our own values and priorities.

Each one of them may seem insignificant, but if each of these choices takes us a little further away from living what's most important to us, then the cumulative effect is no small thing.

As with any of the leadership disciplines, working with time is just the tip of the iceberg that could be called "What's Most Important in Life." How we choose to live every day reflects our deepest values, priorities, and beliefs, even when these are largely unconscious. One of the core requirements of being a leader is to do the work needed to bring these into consciousness and then act from that place of choice on a daily basis.

Chapter 12
Supporting the Growth of Others

Introduction

Although all of the disciplines and practices of leadership are important in their own way, supporting the growth of others is at the essence of what leadership is. By definition, leadership entails relationships with other people. The very notion of leadership implies both a responsibility to others as well as a sense that the leader has more experience, vision, or motivation than do his/her constituents. Therefore, a central aspect of the work of leadership is to support the growth of others.

Why is it so critical to support the growth of others? One pragmatic answer is this: Do you want to be one hundred years old and still hanging in there? Or would you rather be enjoying your senior years, confident that the people you helped bring along are carrying on the work you began? Right this minute, I can think of several people of my generation or older who are getting desperate to relinquish some of their commitments, to slow their pace just a bit, but who don't dare for fear that what they have brought into existence will collapse the moment they pull back. That's not what any of us really wants, but we don't always have a solid plan to keep from ending up in this position.

Supporting the growth of others is also critical because there are a multitude of issues calling for leadership. Each and every leader needs to take on the responsibility to support the growth of others, along with whatever leadership work he/she is directly engaged in.

Another reason to support the growth of others is that there are many roles needed to accomplish the work of leadership, and none of us can do it all. In addition to the out-front leader, there's also the second in command, the person who deals with the details, the individual who cares for and tends to others. If you are in a leadership role and you only focus on "your work" without supporting other people to grow and develop within some of these other roles, there will be many gaps.

In spite of how central this responsibility is, my experience suggests that it is an aspect of leadership easily neglected amidst day-to-day challenges. You have probably heard (and perhaps said this yourself), "It's easier to do it myself than to teach someone how to do it." Leadership takes as strong a commitment to support others to grow as it does to engage in the work of leadership itself.

Lately, I have been thinking a lot about the idea of leaving a legacy. Not surprisingly, it wasn't a preoccupation of mine until fairly recently, although I've always seen supporting the growth of others as both a value and a commitment. For those of us who work in the "people business," supporting the growth of others actually *is* our legacy. I am unlikely to leave buildings, parks, or companies behind. Instead, I aspire to instill in as many people as I can what I've learned in my life. That is what I see as my legacy.

Whose development might you support?

How does one identify people whose development might be supported? The main thing is to support people you want to help on their leadership journey, people interested in taking on leadership roles. A critical aspect of this is motivation, as discussed earlier in the book, is to pay attention to what people are drawn to. Where does someone come to life, perk up, volunteer for something, and then follow through? Motivation is a huge factor in identifying people to support. Dissatisfaction with the status quo is an indicator of motivation—if you can help the person to create a vision of a desired future and then work with them to identify the first few steps. However, if over time the person continues to complain about how bad things are but fails to identify some areas that can be transformed, then you may need to work with that person about being stuck in a victim role. Or you may decide that you don't want to invest in supporting this person.

Openness to learning is another big consideration. A person who already "knows it all" is unlikely to have the humility it takes to be a student. There's a story from the Zen Buddhist tradition that goes like this: "A learned man once went to a Zen master to inquire about Zen. As the Zen master talked, the learned man would frequently interrupt him with remarks like 'Oh yes, we have that too' and so forth. Finally the Zen master stopped talking and began to serve tea to the learned man; however, he kept on pouring, and the teacup overflowed. 'Enough! No more can go into the cup!' the learned man interrupted. 'Indeed, I see,' answered the Zen master. 'If you do not first empty your cup, how can you taste my cup of tea?'"[42]

Follow-through is critically important if you are investing your time, energy, and wisdom in another's development. Why would you want to commit to bringing someone along if they cannot be counted on? Of course, things happen and people sometimes must default. But if you detect a pattern of commitment without follow-through, you're responsible to hold that person accountable. If, after time, the results are not forthcoming, some serious questioning about whether this person deserves your support is in order.

It's not so important that the person has complete confidence in him/herself. After all, does anyone? Rather, you want to look for someone whose explicit or implicit motto is "feel the fear, but do it anyway," someone whose motivation to make a difference is stronger than their self-doubts.

How exactly does one support the growth of others? As parents, you know that child-raising involves creating "containers for growth" that both challenge and support your children. You help a child learn to swim, ride a bike, or walk by helping them to feel safe and relatively confident at the beginning and then gradually opening up more and more space so the child can act independently—while still being there to support her when she hits her edge. It's much the same process in supporting the growth of others into leadership roles. Of course, this is easier said than done with both children and adults.

PRACTICAL CONSIDERATIONS FOR SUPPORTING THE GROWTH OF OTHERS

The following are some of the practical strategies I have learned over the years to support the growth of others.

USE AN INDIVIDUAL APPROACH

Not everyone learns the same way or grows from the same challenges. For example, one of my coaching clients is director of a nonprofit organization. She wants to support her leadership team to take more initiative and responsibility. Up until now, her approach has been to do what worked for her: Tell people what needs to change and ask them if they have any ideas about how to bring about that change. So far, no one has stepped up to the plate, and she's frustrated with them and with herself. We've explored her personal motivation to find solutions to the problems she confronts. She realized that, for her, it's all about serving others and challenging herself to solve problems. She had assumed those were underlying motivations for everyone.

Since our discussion, she has started paying more attention to what motivates individual members of her team and has then tried to present growth opportunities to them in ways that resonate for each of them. For some people, getting a chance to work collaboratively with others is a huge motivation. For others, being recognized as competent is a source of motivation. One of her staff really took pride in figuring something out on her own, whether or not she was recognized by others. It was only when this leader realized that sources of motivation vary that she could begin to create opportunities to support their growth.

Supporting the growth of others requires seeing the potential in each person—maybe even more clearly than they see it in themselves—and crafting opportunities for them to step into that potential. Knowing that there is someone out there who really believes in you is a huge comfort for people as they begin to move out of their comfort zones—not an unrealistic belief but one that is grounded in really knowing the person and what they are capable of. Throughout my life, I have risen to leadership challenges because people I respect have believed that I would succeed, even when I had my own doubts. Their belief in me served as a safety net when I stepped out onto that high-wire.

Yet supporting others also means knowing where people lack potential and directing them away from those areas. Why would someone want to keep trying to get good at something that they just don't have an aptitude for? That's a recipe for frustration. In *First Break All the Rules*, Marcus Buckingham describes these as "nontalents."

He writes, "A nontalent is a mental wasteland. It is a behavior that always seems to be a struggle. It is a thrill that is never felt. It is an insight recurrently missed … You have many more nontalents than you do talents, but most of them are irrelevant. You should ignore them."[43] As someone who is focused on supporting the growth of others, put your energy into helping people "become more of who they already are" rather than attempting to acquire capabilities around their nontalents. It will be more satisfying and productive for everyone.

CREATE ROOM FOR PEOPLE TO SHINE

How can people grow new capabilities if there's no room for them to apply their talent? If the existing leaders have everything covered, how can new people move into leadership roles? Sometimes this happens because existing leaders are stretched so thin that they fear everything will come crashing down if they open up a space for people to grow into. There's also the fear that someone new will usurp the power of existing leaders, outshine them, or make them look bad. That sounds like an unsavory thought, but it's human to feel threatened when one senses someone breathing down one's back. It may be entirely irrational and counter to one's espoused commitment to supporting the growth of others. A colleague of mine challenges leaders not only to support the growth of others but to help others become twice as successful as they themselves were. If that makes your heart beat a little faster, you're in the right territory!

MAKE A DEVELOPMENTAL PATH

Give people assignments that are challenging but can be accomplished successfully. Nothing succeeds like success! If, as a leader, you want to bring other people along, you will have the best results if you create a sequence of increasingly challenging opportunities that people can grow into. For example, if you are helping someone grow into a role that requires them to speak in front of others, a first step might be for them to help you prepare an outline of a presentation you will be delivering. You can give them helpful advice and instruction without the fear that they will also have to be in the spotlight. Next time, you might invite the person to make a few comments in the midst of a presentation you are giving. Then perhaps they might participate in a panel presentation. Finally, the person might be ready to develop and deliver the whole presentation. You always want to be thinking about creating those "containers for growth" mentioned earlier. And at any point along the sequence, it might turn out that the person has reached their highest potential with that particular challenge.

OFFER HONEST AND SUPPORTIVE FEEDBACK

One important way to support another's growth is by planning what they are going to do and then reviewing how it went. Help the person focus on what they learned that will enable them to improve next time. Giving this kind of feedback can be challenging. On the one hand, you want the person to feel supported, encouraged, and open to there being a next time. On the other hand, it's likely the person could use some feedback from someone they respect and who has their best interests at heart. Try to make the feedback specific and behavioral (something one can observe): "When you led that meeting, you only looked at the right side of the room. At least two people to your left looked like they wanted to speak, but you didn't notice them. Next time, make sure to look all around the room." Also offer ideas or suggestions of things that can be tried the next time.

HOLD PEOPLE ACCOUNTABLE

Accountability is a key to trusting relationships. There is nothing that undermines a relationship more than people who do not honor their commitments. In fact, this is probably the biggest single contributor to difficult conversations. Why wait until accountability is violated to have the conversation? Why not set clear expectations up front? It seems like good common sense, yet when it comes to holding people accountable, we are often quite "squishy." We vaguely ask, "Would anyone volunteer to hold the next meeting at their house?" and then we get frustrated when no one offers.

One of the most effective tools for increasing accountability is a simple protocol called "Requests and Promises." If you want to ask someone to do something, you might say "I request that you (fill in the blanks)." The person then gets to accept, decline, or counteroffer. Counteroffers may involve negotiating more time, more resources, more support, or possibly a smaller scope of responsibility. Before agreeing, it's a good idea to be clear about exactly what the action is and by when. Once you both agree on what is going to happen, the recipient of the request promises to fulfill the terms of the agreement. You can then hold that person accountable for what they promised.

Here's an example:

> Parent to teenaged son: "Joe, I request that you clean your room by 6:00 p.m. today."
> Son: "Aw, Mom, I planned to pay basketball all afternoon. Could you give me until noon tomorrow?" (counteroffer, negotiating more time)
> Parent: "Yes, I can accept that, but you also need to put away your folded laundry in your dresser drawers. Will you promise to do that?" (counter-counteroffer, enlarging the scope of responsibility)
> Son: "If I have to, yes … I promise."

Of course this scenario is very simplistic: a real-life negotiation with a teenager would probably involve setting precise criteria about what "clean" looks like and a much more extended negotiation, perhaps ending without the promise. But you get the idea.

One thing that contributes to a lack of accountability is what are called weak requests where you hint at something you would like done. This is often done without specifying what, by when, or by whom you'd like it done. ("Can't somebody give me some help around here?") Using the Requests and Promises protocol is one way to step up accountability.

GIVE SPECIFICS ABOUT THE OUTCOME BUT NOT THE METHODS

This is one of the classic principles for effective delegation, but it's often ignored. We can be so attached to our way of doing something that we forget it's not the only way, nor is it necessarily the best way. There are many different approaches to reaching the same outcome, and if we insist that others do things our way, we may lose an opportunity to support another person's growth. For example, one mother I talked to complained that no one in the family helped her around the house. She had tried to get her husband and children to help without much success. The problem was that she was completely attached to her way of doing things and wouldn't accept any variation. We discussed what her *real* priority was—getting help or having the dishwasher stacked exactly the way she did it. Although she had initially thought her priority was to get help, she was completely stuck on having the dishwasher just so. No matter how silly she knew it to be, she was not prepared to relax her standards, even though it meant continuing to do that task herself. Where are *you* unwilling to bend? And what's the cost—to you and to someone you're trying to develop?

Of course there are those occasions where you don't have leeway: a document needs to be prepared using a certain format or a meeting needs to be run using certain procedures. If that is the case, let the person know what the outcomes are, as well as what is nonnegotiable in terms of how it gets done. Pay attention to your assumptions about what is nonnegotiable however. Is it your idea of how it needs to be done, or is it really written in stone? By insisting that things be done a certain way, you might be discouraging the growth of someone else's creativity as well as forcing them to do a task in a way that does not come naturally to them.

WHAT IMPEDES PEOPLE FROM TAKING RESPONSIBILITY?

So, you've identified someone you'd like to bring along. You think they have the right combination of qualities, and you reach out to them with an invitation. They refuse! What's going on here?

Let's get the clearest reason out of the way. The person has other priorities, and his motivation is not as strong as you thought it was. It's actually a real advantage to find this out early on, rather than investing in that person and having him later discover that he isn't in it for the long haul. It's also possible that someone is slightly motivated, and having a series of small, successful assignments could increase that motivation. For example, someone is willing to give your daughter with disabilities a ride to a meeting but isn't currently inclined to support your daughter in more extensive ways. The ride is a good start: Relationships are being formed, your daughter's engaging qualities are being discovered, and maybe in the future the person's motivation to support your daughter in other ways may strengthen ... or not! A ride is still a positive thing in itself.

Sometimes people decline out of fear. Fear that they won't know what to do, fear that they won't measure up, or any of the fears described in chapter 2 might apply here. Almost every leadership opportunity I've been offered has been accompanied by massive and unreasonable fear. Knowing that other people have confidence in me has been the only reason I've "felt the fear and done it anyway." When you are in a position to support the growth of others, offer that gift of confidence, but not in a generic way. Don't just say, "I know you can do it." People interpret that as an expectation, and it often results in even more fear. Instead, give people specifics about why you believe in them. What qualities do you see in them that they may not fully claim? What track record of accomplishments are they overlooking that caused you to think they were worth investing in?

Offer to support the person in areas where they feel weak. The combination of moral support ("You can run any ideas or concerns by me") with actual practical support ("I can help you set up a bookkeeping system") can work wonders when a person is motivated but lacking in confidence.

Team the person up with others who are more experienced, especially people who will offer both practical help and encouragement. And if it just isn't working out, pay attention to the possibility that you may be pushing the person too hard or have misidentified their potential. There is no point in people being miserable and not accomplishing what you've committed to.

HOW MIGHT YOU BE INADVERTENTLY SUPPRESSING THE GROWTH OF OTHERS?

Earlier we addressed some of the challenges leaders face in creating room for people to shine. As a leader, in spite of your espoused desire to bring people along, you may be inadvertently sabotaging yourself. Here are some of the ways it can happen.

Being too perfect yourself: If you can do everything, why do you need other people? The whole idea is to create room! Pay attention to those areas where you *could* do something and perhaps have had to do it in the past when there was no one else to help. Maybe you've always hated recruiting people to work on projects, but you had to do it because there was no one else around. Find someone who loves to do that, and turn them loose. Initially it may feel strange, like you've abdicated responsibility or given away a part of yourself, but if you think of this as being for the benefit of those you are bringing along and not as something selfish, it can be a little easier.

Not allowing for a learning curve: Once we become accomplished at something, it's easy to forget how long it took for us to learn. It can be frustrating to see people struggle, and it's also time-consuming. Before you turn something over to someone, go over in your mind what the steps of mastery might be and how much time it might take to attain mastery. Keep in mind the rule of thumb is that it takes 10,000 hours to achieve true mastery in any skill, from composing symphonies to playing tennis. Think of your own experience and talk to other people. What would be the stages or phases of that learning curve? That will help you be patient, and it will give your protégé some guidance about where they are on their learning curve.

Micromanaging: One earlier suggestion was to "give specifics about the outcome but not the methods." It can be a real turnoff to feel as if someone else is looking over your shoulder, evaluating everything you do in light of their own way of doing things. It's easy to see how someone might decide that it's easier to let you do it than it is to learn precisely how you want them to do it. While there is nothing wrong with having guidelines, when you find yourself micromanaging, you might want to ask yourself whether you really want to turn that task or project over to someone else or if you'd rather find something else to let go of.

Giving people mixed messages about their capacity: This can be done in varied and subtle ways. Micromanaging is one way of communicating the message that you don't have confidence in someone else. Imagine you've just written your first press release, and you hand it proudly to the leader of your group. The next day, he hands it back to you, marked up in red pencil and practically rewritten. Although he may not have intended this, your self-confidence is likely to be undermined, and you may wonder whether you're capable of writing another press release. While developmental feedback is useful, as a leader it's important to think through how it might be received and to balance the support for growth with affirmation of the person's capacity.

Another way to communicate mixed messages is to deny someone the opportunity to take on a new challenge when they feel ready for it. Of course, you don't want to hand the assignment over to them without any preparation or safeguards. But it can really undermine someone's sense of their own capability to have a person they look up to (you!) appear to have doubts about their ability to take the next step. If you genuinely believe someone is not ready, be specific about why you believe that and what it would take to become ready. This feedback is likely to be better received than a sweeping statement like, "You're not ready."

This chapter has addressed a set of practices that are central to the long-term effectiveness of your leadership. Unless you pay attention to bringing other people along—on a regular basis and not at the end of your leadership career—the important work you are engaged in will ultimately run out of momentum. As families and advocates of people with disabilities, this is not something you can afford to do. One of the perennial questions asked by families is, "What will happen to my son or daughter when I'm no longer around?" Supporting the growth of others—early and often—is perhaps the best response to that question.

CONCLUSION: KEY POINTS TO TAKE AWAY

At the time of this writing, I will have been working on this book for almost a decade. It's been a long journey. At many points I've wondered whether I would ever finish. Writing, like leadership, requires a huge amount of motivation. For me, the strongest sources of motivation have been the families who've regularly asked, "When is your book coming out?" Knowing that there are people interested in what I have to say and counting on me to fulfill my promise is what has kept me working away at this, no matter how bogged down I've gotten. This too is like leadership; what we might have difficulty doing just for ourselves somehow becomes possible when we know other people are counting on us.

I'd like to close by reiterating several of the main points I've tried to make throughout the book:

1. Leadership can be exercised by anyone motivated to make a difference.
2. At the same time, skillful leadership requires discipline and practice over time.
3. Leadership is a collective activity that also requires individual responsibility and accountability.
4. Leadership, as Ron Heifetz writes, "requires the courage to face failures daily." By definition, being a leader means you're in uncharted territory.
5. While leadership carries many risks, the fundamental question is: why *not* lead? As my yoga instructor Amy said, "You can choose the highest (principle) or not; life is still going to be hard."

May our paths cross on this challenging, rewarding, and joyful journey.

About the Author

Deborah Reidy has worked in the human service field since 1976, with the majority of her work aimed at creating conditions for people with disabilities to be valued, contributing members of their communities. At the age of twenty-four, she founded a residential agency serving some of the most severely disabled people who lived outside institutions at the time. She then founded an innovative program, Education for Community Initiatives (ECI), which offered education and consultation to community members and the staff of human service agencies in their efforts to include people with disabilities in all aspects of community life. Since the late 1970s, she had been a leader in the disability field, primarily in the area of social integration, community membership, and stigma reduction.

Upon leaving ECI in 1993, Ms. Reidy joined the Massachusetts Department of Mental Retardation (now Department of Developmental Services, DDS) as Director of Training and Development. As Director of Training and Development, she was responsible for organizing a system of training for many thousands of service workers, families, board members, and others. One of the very biggest needs was a coordinated strategy to support the leadership development of the staff, families, and service recipients affiliated with the agency. Ms. Reidy played a key role in designing and delivering leadership development programs in Massachusetts and has continued to do so since the mid-90s. This intensive exposure has presented great opportunities to refine her thinking about leadership in the human service field and to review and incorporate relevant works from other thinkers.

In 2001, she became involved with the Society for Organizational Learning (SoL), a membership organization founded by Peter Senge, author of *The Fifth Discipline* and other notable books. She became active in SoL and continued to incorporate the most updated thinking and writing on leadership into her work with people with disabilities, their families, and their allies. From 1996 to 2002, she directed an agency called Cornerstone, which was a center for leadership and community development in the disability field. Its purpose was to provide education and support for practices aimed at enabling individuals with disabilities to be valued members of the communities in which they lived and worked. She left Cornerstone in October of 2002 to develop her own consulting business in the area of leadership and organizational development, Reidy Associates.

In addition to her extensive training and management experience, Ms. Reidy has published many articles, book chapters, and reports. She has led hundreds of training events, planning sessions, and retreats; has conducted numerous evaluations and action research projects; and has provided executive and team coaching. Ms. Reidy holds an undergraduate degree in sociology and a masters' degree in Adult Education and is a certified coach.

She lives in Massachusetts, with her husband, Jim, and their two Himalayan cats.

BIBLIOGRAPHY

Bellman, Geoffrey. *Getting Things Done When You are Not in Charge.* New York: Simon & Schuster, 1992.

Block, Peter. *The Answer to How Is Yes: Acting on What Matters.* San Francisco: Berrett-Koehler Publishers, Inc., 2002.

Breen, Bill. "What's Your Intuition?," *Fast Company,* retrieved from www.fastcompany.com/magazine/38/klein.html?page=0%2C2.

Bronson, Po, and Ashley Merryman. "The Creativity Crisis." *Newsweek,* July 19, 2010.

Buckingham, Marcus, and Curt Coffman. *First, Break All the Rules.* New York: Simon & Schuster, 1999.

Buechner, Frederick. *The Longing for Home: Recollections & Reflections.* San Francisco: HarperCollins, 1996.

Canabou, Christine. "Fast Talk: Hail Global Citizens!" *Fast Company,* 78:61, 2004.

Carlson, Richard. *Don't Sweat the Small Stuff ... and It's All Small Stuff.* New York: Hyperion, 1997.

Chödrön, Pema. *Start Where You Are: A Guide to Compassionate Living.* Boston: Shambhala Publications, 1994.

Clark, Don. "Communication and Leadership," *Big Dog & Little Dog's Performance Juxtaposition,* retrieved from www.nwlink .com/~donclark/leader/leadcom.html.

Cooperrider, David, Diana Whitney, and Jacqueline Stavros. *Appreciative Inquiry Handbook*. Bedford Heights, Ohio: Lakeshore Publishers, 2003.

Cottrell, David. *Monday Morning Leadership*. Dallas: CornerStone Leadership Institute, 2002.

Covey, Stephen. *The 7 Habits of Highly Successful People*. New York: Simon and Schuster, 1989.

Dannemiller Tyson Associates. *Whole-Scale Change: Unleashing the Magic in Organizations*. San Francisco: Berrett-Koehler Publishers, 2000.

Gladwell, Malcolm. *The Tipping Point: How Little Things Can Make a Big Difference*. Boston: Back Bay Books, 2002.

Gottman, John, and Joan DeClaire. *The Relationship Cure*. New York: Three Rivers Press, 2001.

Gottman, John, and Nan Silver. *The Seven Principles for Making Marriage Work*. New York: Three Rivers Press, 1999.

Hammond, Sue Annis. *The Thin Book of Appreciative Inquiry*. Plano, Texas: Thin Book Publishing, 1998.

Hargadon, Andrew. "The Trouble with Out-of-the-Box Thinking: Andrew Hargadon on Continuity and Its Critical Role in the Innovation Process," *ACM Portal*, retrieved from www.acm.org /ubiquity/interviews/v4i30_hargadon.html.

Heifetz, Ronald. *Leadership without Easy Answers*. Cambridge, Massachusetts: Belknap Press of Harvard University Press, 1994.

Heifetz, Ronald, and Marty Linsky. *Leadership on the Line: Staying Alive through the Dangers of Leading*. Boston: Harvard Business School Press, 2002.

Kouzes, James, and Barry Posner. *The Leadership Challenge: How to Get Extraordinary Things Done in Organizations*. San Francisco: Jossey-Bass, 1987.

Loehr, Jim, and Tony Schwartz. *The Power of Full Engagement*. New York: The Free Press, 2003.

Myss, Caroline. *Anatomy of the Spirit: The Seven Stages of Power and Healing.* New York: Three Rivers Press, 1996.

Palmer, Parker. *The Courage to Teach: Exploring the Inner Landscape of a Teacher's Life.* San Francisco: Jossey-Bass, 1998.

Patterson, Kerry, et al. *Crucial Confrontations.* New York: McGraw Hill, 2005.

Piercy, Marge. *Circles on the Water: Selected Poems.* New York: Alfred Knopf, 1994.

Rilke, Rainer Maria. *Letters to a Young Poet.* Translated by Stephen Mitchell. New York: Random House, 1984.

Seligman, Martin. *Authentic Happiness: Using the New Positive Psychology to Realize Your Potential for Lasting Fulfillment.* New York: Free Press, 2002.

Senge, Peter. *The Fifth Discipline.* New York: Currency Doubleday, 1990.

Senge, Peter, et al. *The Fifth Discipline Fieldbook.* New York: Currency Doubleday, 1994.

Wycoff, Joyce, *Mind mapping: Your Personal Guide to Exploring Creativity and Problem-Solving.* New York: Berkley Books, 1991.

ENDNOTES

1. Block, *The Answer to How Is Yes: Acting on What Matters,* 42.
2. Bellman, *Getting Things Done When You Are Not in Charge,* 19.
3. Matthew 22:39.
4. Palmer, *The Courage to Teach,* 169.
5. Buechner, *The Longing for Home,* 140.
6. Seligman, *Authentic Happiness,* 66.
7. Heifetz and Linsky, *Leadership on the Line,* 2.
8. Heifetz and Linsky, *Leadership on the Line,* 3.
9. Rilke, *Letters to a Young Poet,* 82.
10. Cooperrider, Whitney, & Stavros, *Appreciative Inquiry Handbook,* xiii.
11. Hammond, *The Thin Book of Appreciative Inquiry,* 26–27.
12. Cooperrider, Whitney, & Stavros, *Appreciative Inquiry Handbook,* 12.
13. Canabou, "Fast Talk: Hail Global Citizens!," *Fast Company,* 78:61.
14. Senge, *The Fifth Discipline,* 225.
15. Kouzes and Posner, *The Leadership Challenge,* 87–92.
16. Dannemiller Tyson Associates, *Whole-scale Change: Unleashing the Magic in Organizations,* 16.
17. Kouzes and Posner, *The Leadership Challenge,* 93.
18. Breen, "What's Your Intuition?," *Fast Company,* retrieved from www.fastcompany.com/magazine/38/klein.html?page=0%2C2.
19. Senge, *The Fifth Discipline,* 150.
20. Piercy, *Circles on the Water,* 128.
21. Heifetz, *Leadership Without Easy Answers,* 73–84.
22. Heifetz, *Leadership Without Easy Answers,* 22.
23. Gladwell, *The Tipping Point,* back cover.
24. Heifetz, *Leadership Without Easy Answers,* 275.
25. Carlson, *Don't Sweat the Small Stuff,* 171.

26. Chödrön, *Start Where You Are,* 89.

27. Myss, *Anatomy of the Spirit,* 40.

28. Bronson and Merryman, "The Creativity Crisis," *Newsweek,* 45.

29. Hargadon, "The Trouble with Out-of-the-Box Thinking," *ACM Portal,* retrieved from www.acm.org/ubiquity/interviews /v4i30_hargadon.html

30. Wycoff, *Mind mapping,* 42.

31. Clark, *Communication and Leadership,* retrieved from www .nwlink.com/~donclark/leader/leadcom.html

32. Covey, *The 7 Habits of Highly Successful People,* 237.

33. Gottman and DeClaire, *The Relationship Cure,* 81–82.

34. Patterson, Grenny, McMillan, and Switzler, *Crucial Confrontations,* 25.

35. Gottman and Silver, *The Seven Principles for Making Marriage Work,* 26.

36. Heifetz and Linsky, *Leadership on the Line,* 101.

37. Senge, et al., *The Fifth Discipline Fieldbook,* 389.

38. Patterson, Grenny, McMillan, and Switzler, *Crucial Confrontations,* 90.

39. *Thomas Killman Conflict Mode Instrument,* retrieved from http://en.wikipedia.org/wiki/Thomas_Kilmann_Conflict_Mode _Instrument.

40. Cottrell, *Monday Morning Leadership,* 36.

41. Loehr and Schwartz, *The Power of Full Engagement,* 5.

42. Retrieved from Zen Stories, http://w.eternalvigilance.org/ma /stories/#empty, January 21, 2008.

43. Buckingham and Coffman, *First, Break All the Rules,* 167.